today's beach houses

Edition 2005

Author: Pilar Chueca
Publisher: Carles Broto
Editorial Coordinator: Jacobo Krauel
Graphic designer & production: Dimitris Kottas
Text: contributed by the architects, edited by Amber Ockrassa and
Marta Rojals

© Carles Broto i Comerma
Jonqueres, 10, 1-5
08003 Barcelona, Spain
Tel.: +34 93 301 21 99
 Fax: +34-93-301 00 21
E-mail: info@linksbooks.net
www. linksbooks.net

today's beach houses

INTRODUCTION

Water has always been a major attraction and a popular site for locating residences. The sea has been a great source of wealth and resources, and has led to the emergence and development of many towns and cities all over the world.

At the present time, the aquatic world is also an ideal framework in which to spend one's holidays or to lead a peaceful life in a landscape that maintains a close dialogue with the individual. Water is at the same time soothing and uncontrollable, involving immensity and variation. It acts as a mirror that multiplies the landscape, it illuminates spaces with its reflections and it contributes a countless range of shades that provide its admirers with a great variety of sensations.

This book presents some of the schemes located on the coasts of the earth. They show the efforts of their designers to conceive an architecture that is elegant, appropriate to its environment and able to provide its inhabitants with the necessary comfort and security to enjoy a stimulating interaction with nature. These unusual works are located on seas and oceans but do not damage their idyllic image of natural paradises. Fortunately, respect for the environment and care to avoid aggressive visual impacts are increasingly influential factors in the design of buildings that are intended as something more than simple inhabitable spaces. These buildings are dream houses for many people, the refuge to which they can retreat from the stress of modern life. The architects organize the spaces to take full advantage of their location and to create a dialogue with the interior and the exterior of the building so that the two concepts are often merged into one. The aspects that are given most emphasis by the architects that appear in this selection are the use of appropriate and sturdy materials that can withstand the latent violence of water, the arrangement of elements or structures that provide refreshing shade for hot summer days, the incorporation of pools as elements that benefit both the inhabitants and the dwellings, and the careful selection of colors and textures for the facades. Each architect deals with these elements in their own way, showing their distinctive touch and representing the demands of the clients and the site. This is an architecture created for a blue world in which the sea determines the final configuration and in which the distant harmonious horizon seems to be closer than ever.

Tadao Ando

4 x 4 House

Kobe, Hyogo, Japan

The site is a beachfront facing the Seto Inland Sea. On the opposite shore 4 kilometers away lies Hokudan-town on the Awaji Island, the epicenter of the 1995 Great Hanshin Earthquake. To the east stretches the Akashi strait Bridge. This location has presented the architect with the opportunity to develop the project by looking at the Awaji Island where he had been given the chance to work on various projects such as the Water Temple and Yumebutai, and at the Akashi Bridge, a demonstration of Japan's world-class construction technology.

The site is subject to erosion by the sea. A good part of the land has already turned into a sandy beach of rare beauty, leaving a mere patch of dry land behind the breakwater.

The four-story tower has a square plan of 4m x 4m, whose uppermost level is a cube 4m on each side that protrudes towards the sea and that is shifted to the east side by one meter, thus saving the space for stairs. The landscape framed within this cube is a panorama sweeping over the Inland Sea, the Awaji Island and the Awaji Bridge where, for the client who makes a living in this region as well as for the architect, thoughts and memories of the earthquake are embedded. The ground floor accommodates the entrance, bathroom, and lavatory; the second floor the bedroom; the third floor the study, the fourth floor the living room and kitchen.

After the completion of the house a man who had occasionally visited it rented the adjacent land from the owner of the 4 x 4 house and asked the architect to design him a house. The architect is now considering the possibility of building a house symmetrical to the previous one but made of wood instead of concrete.

In the near future, the two houses of "similar shape yet different materials" will sit side by side facing the Inland Sea.

Photographs: Mitsuo Matsuoka

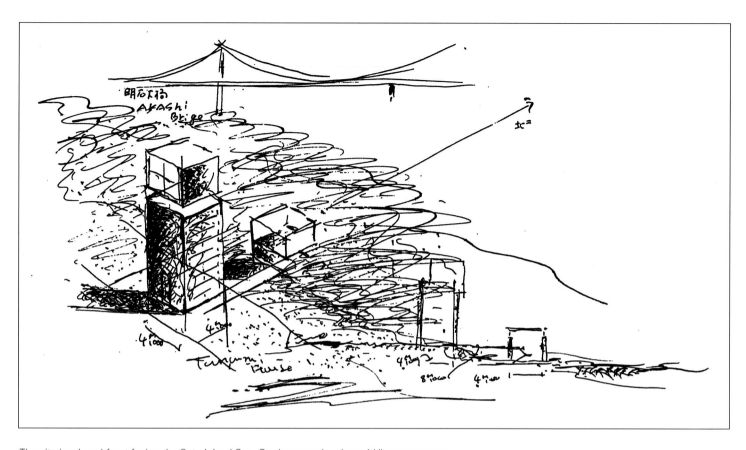

The site is a beachfront facing the Seto Inland Sea. On the opposite shore 4 kilometers away lies Awaji Island, the epicenter of the 1995 Great Hanshin Earthquake, where the architect had been given the chance to work on various projects such as the Water Temple. To the east stretches the Akashi Strait Bridge.

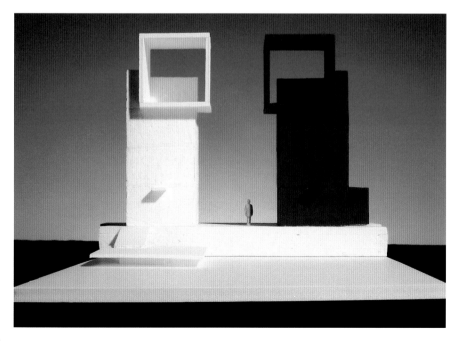
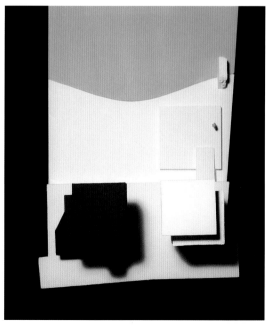

4th floor - living room

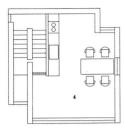

3rd floor - study room

2nd floor - bedroom

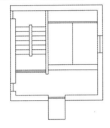

Ground floor - bathroom

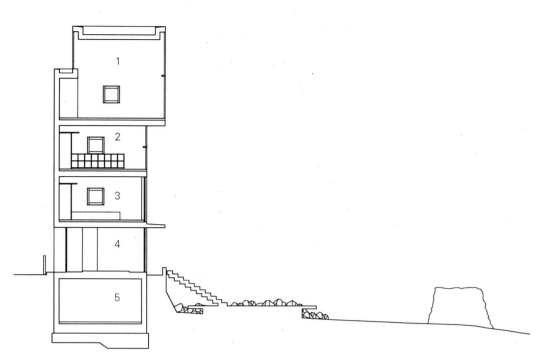

Section
1. Living room
2. Study room
3. Bedroom
4. Entrance
5. Storage

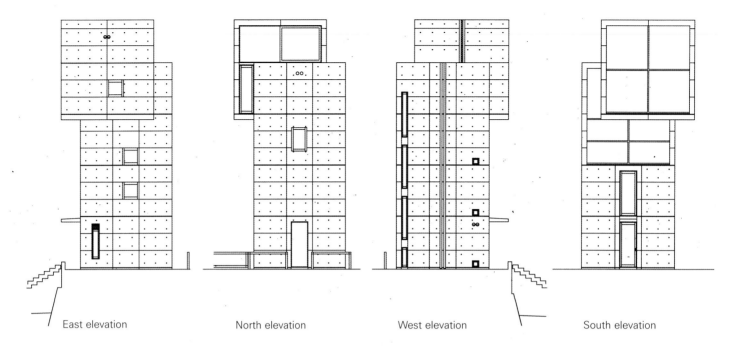

East elevation

North elevation

West elevation

South elevation

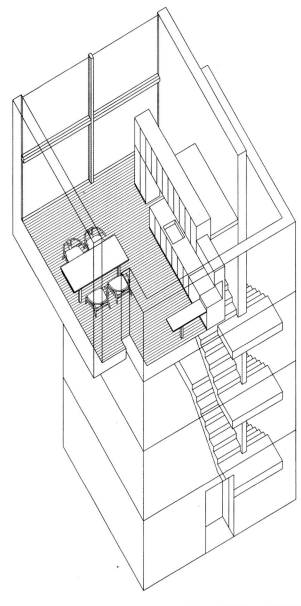

Javier Atardi
House in Las Arenas

Lima, Peru

The project consists of a small house on a coastal plot a hundred kilometers south of Lima. Conceptually, the program explores an elaboration on the uses to which a beach house can be put. Thus, a sort of 'box container' has been created, a complete space that pulls together the living/dining room and the terrace/swimming pool area and that also features a number of diverse elements (both conventional as well as highly unconventional) that allow for multiple functional options.

Architecturally, the box has been perforated along some of its planes in order to achieve an appropriate control of natural light and to guide sight-lines.

The effect of the construction is that of a dynamic interplay of planes and orthogonal volumes, of simple and clearly defined lines, with a certain porosity and internal spatial transparency brought about by the inclusion of large picture windows and uninterrupted paths. The entire length of the building's side walls are somewhat more opaque and the windows become narrow horizontal and vertical strips for preserving a sense of privacy.

White stucco indiscriminately clads both the interior and exterior, creating an atmosphere that adopts the unique quality of light that is so typical of seascapes.

The house has been deliberately 'suspended' over the gardens and thereby incorporates a sense of defying gravity and freedom in the architectonic experience of its inhabitants.

Javier Artadí's studio has sought to incorporate a different architectural typology into the program, with the end goal of increasing the options of what a beach house on the Peruvian coast at the dawn of a new century could possibly be.

Photographs: Alexander Kornhuber

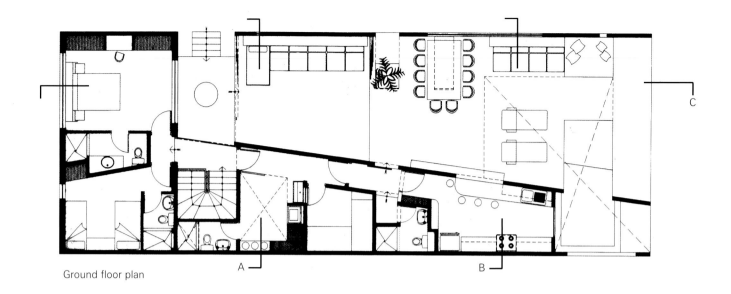

Ground floor plan

A   B   C

Basement floor plan

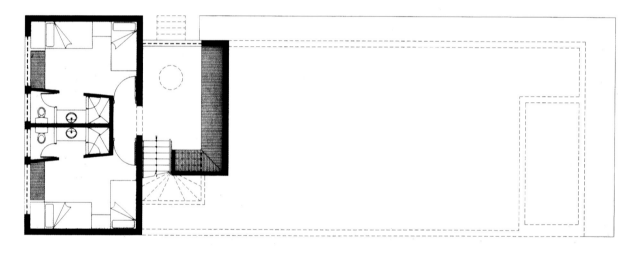

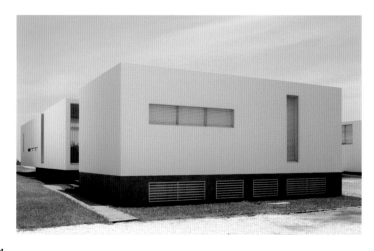

The home is a deliberate reinterpretation for a new century of standard local typologies of what constitutes a beach house.

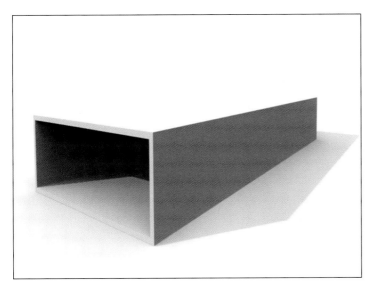

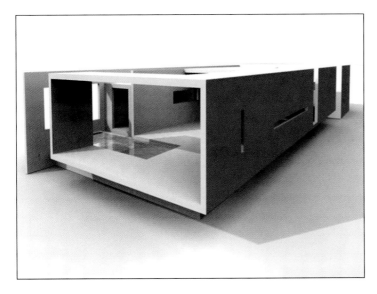

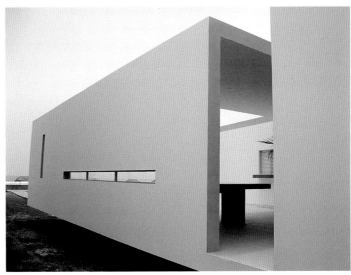

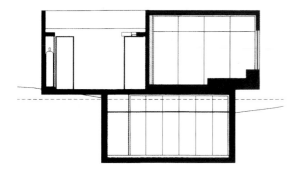

Section A

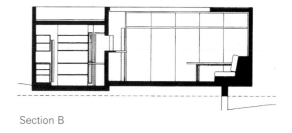

Section B

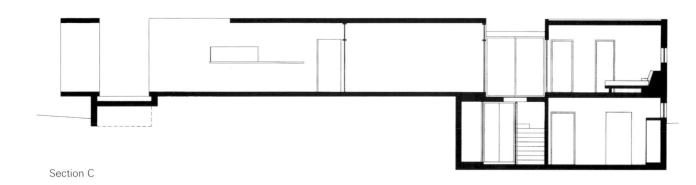

Section C

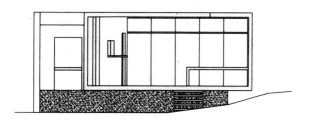

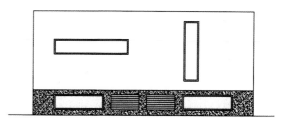

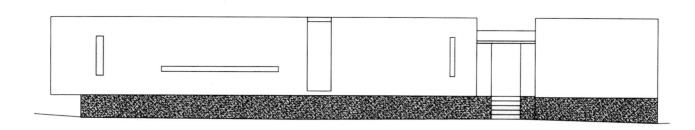

The effect of the construction is that of a dynamic interplay of planes and orthogonal volumes, of simple and clearly defined lines, with a certain porosity and internal spatial transparency, all of which has been meticulously planned and applied.

Jordi Garcés
House in La Fosca

Palamós, Spain

The 'Casa en la Fosca' (literally, 'House in the Dark in Catalan), sits on a 3000-square-meter plot of land on which 630 sqm of landscaped terrain have been set aside for terraces and a solarium. Both of the sectors corresponding to the dwelling and the garden have been established as a unified whole in which the rooms of the home also constitute the areas on the site that are the most shielded from the sun.

A linear volume offers a façade that is mostly closed toward the least advantageous views and to the neighboring buildings; a series of orthogonal bodies of varying lengths emerge from this main linear block in a modular and systematic manner. These secondary volumes are freely molded to the triangular shape of the plot.

The entire program has been laid out on two levels, encompassing 1150 sqm, and includes living rooms, a kitchen/dining room, a master suite and various bedrooms, porches, terraces, pergolas and a solarium. A sort of central vertebra houses the linear stairwell and also groups storage and service spaces along its periphery. On the other side, the wooden terraces stretch toward the sea until reaching the very edge of the land before it gives way to the sea.

Complementary annexes include a pavilion containing a Turkish bath and an exterior jacuzzi with its accompanying machine room. A half-moon shaped storage area completes the buildings and contributes to defining the garden spaces.

The walls, both inside and out, have a stucco finish with a crown of stone. The flooring on the ground level is also in stone, while high-quality natural wood windows, doors and surfaces predominate on the upper floor.

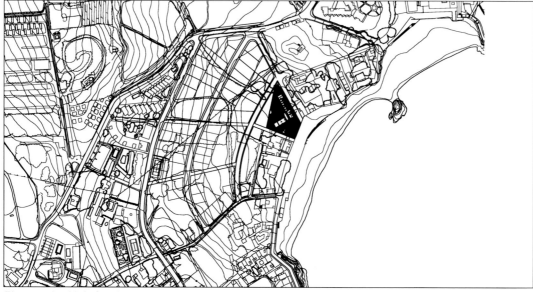

Photographs: Lluís Casals

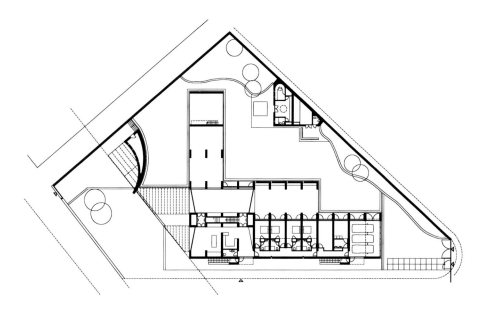

Ground floor plan

0m 4.0 8.0 12.0 16.0 20.0

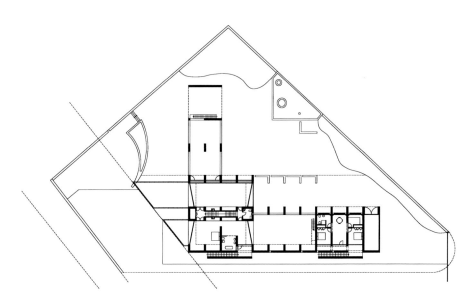

First floor plan

0m 4.0 8.0 12.0 16.0 20.0

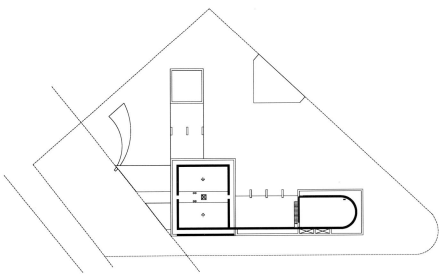

Second floor plan

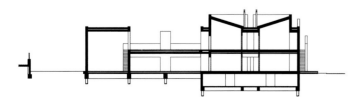
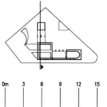

0m 3 6 9 12 15

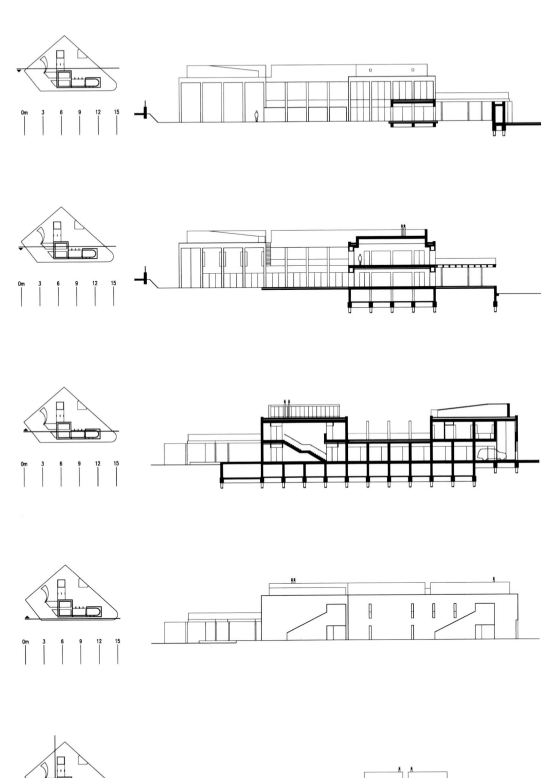

0m   3   6   9   12   15

0m   3   6   9   12   15

0m   3   6   9   12   15

0m   3   6   9   12   15

0m   3   6   9   12   15

Nitsche Arquitectos Associados
House in Barra do Sahy

São Sebastião, São Paolo, Brazil

The architectural team's aim was to build a functional house through a rational construction process, prioritizing promptitude and low cost. In this manner, regular dimensional areas were created on the basis of modular structures. Three modules were arranged linearly for the bedrooms and bathrooms, as well as three other modules for the living and service areas. The articulation between these areas is only made by the external terrace, eliminating the internal circulation, thus optimizing the constructed area and the non-interference of each area.

There were two environmental factors to consider during the design and construction phases: excessive humidity and high temperatures.

In order to prevent the absorption of soil humidity, a concrete platform suspended from the ground was worked into the design; in order to avoid the buildup of air humidity, cross ventilation was enabled in every room. To mitigate the heat, an extended leveled roof that is "loose", corresponding to the house's volume, creates an open space through which the air constantly circulates. The thick eaves shield heavy rain and direct sunlight.

Industrialized materials were chosen that could be assembled on the construction site. For the floor platform, pre-assembled reinforced concrete slab was used; over this level, brick walls made of concrete blocks were built and wooden framework was assembled, all of which is crowned by aluminum thermo-acoustic roof tiles. Aluminum and glass panels were used for the enclosing elements.

The ample space, reinforced by the continuousness of the floor (done in white Sao Tomé stone), as well as the sliding glass panels on both sides, convey a sensation of lightness, where the inner and outer boundaries become diluted.

Photographs: Nelson Kon

Plan

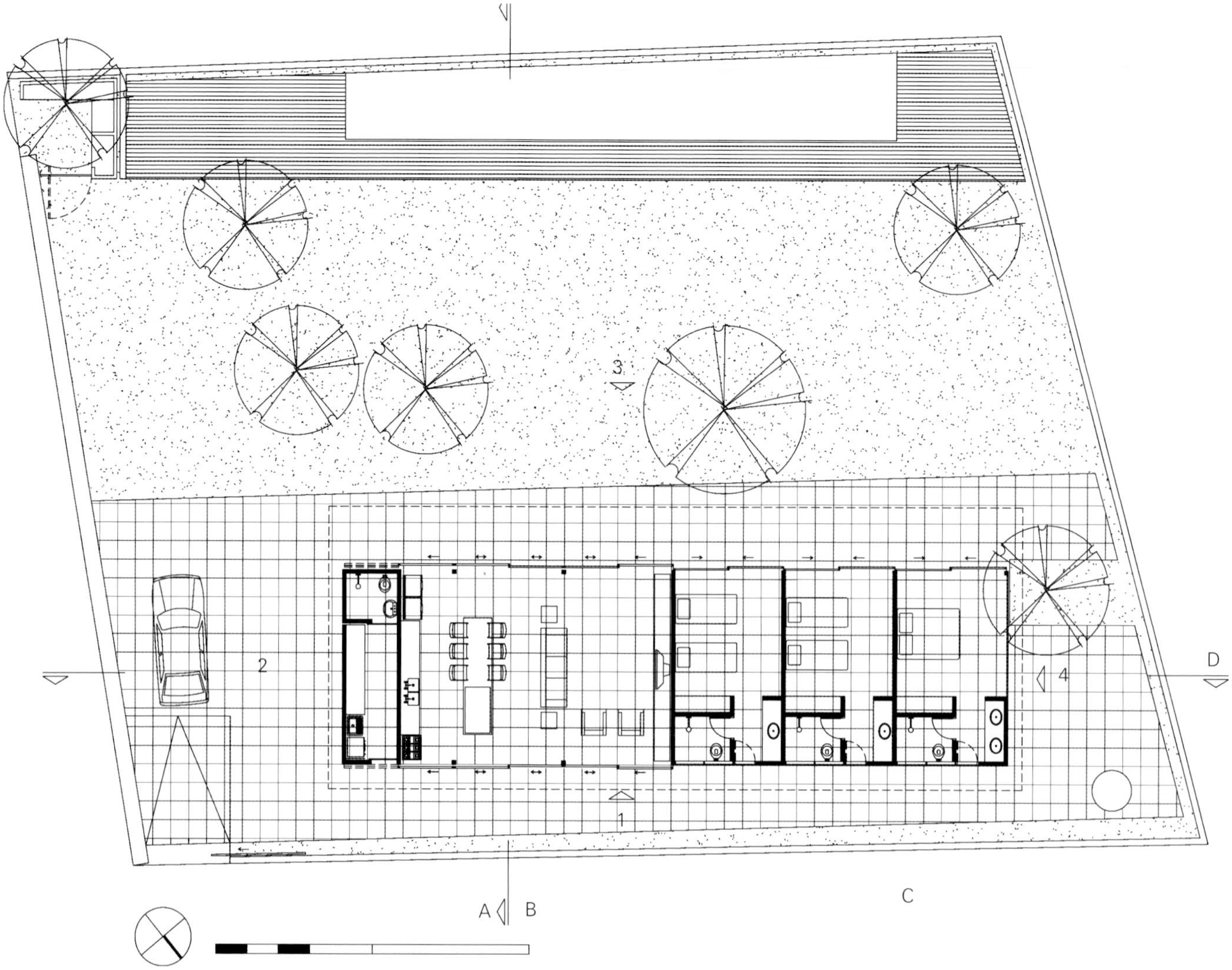

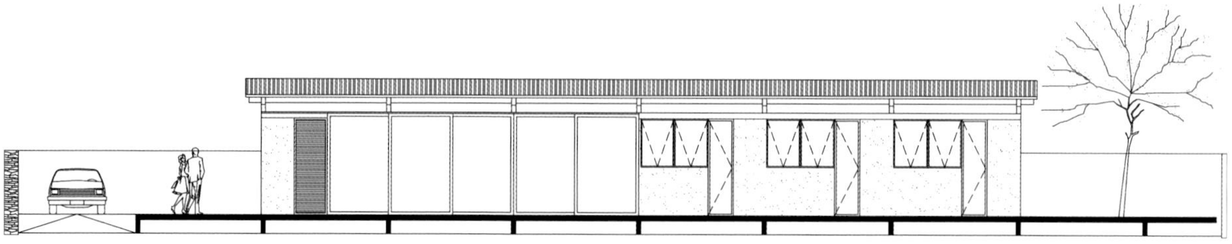

A ◁ B

C

D ▷

3 ▽

4 ◁

2

1 △

Elevation 1

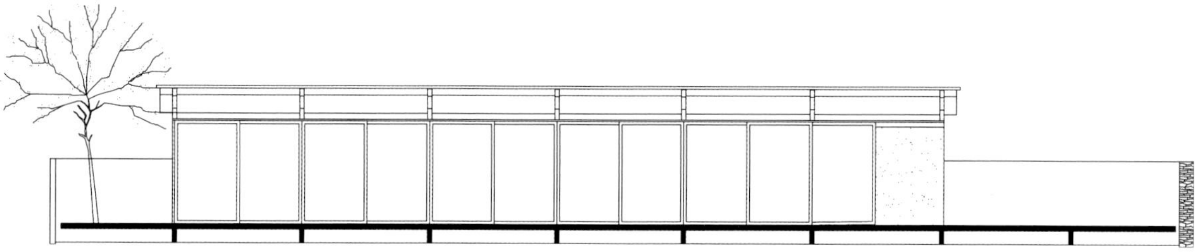

Elevation 3

50

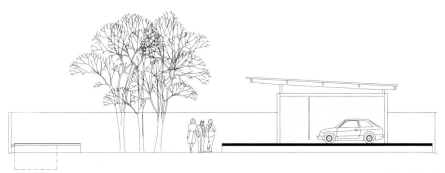

Elevation 2

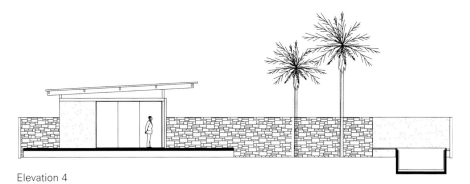

Elevation 4

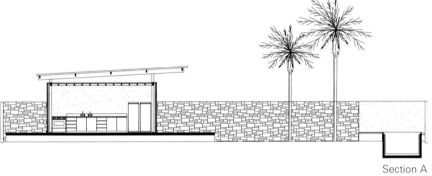

Section A

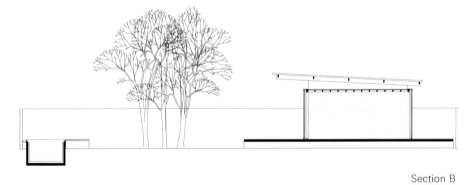

Section B

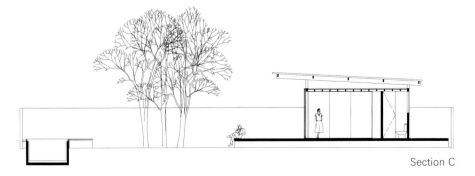

Section C

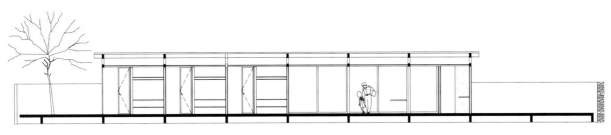

Section D

Dawson Brown Architecture
James-Robertson House

Mackeral Beach, NSW, Australia

Located on a steep, 45 degree, northeast-facing slope on the western foreshores of Pittwater to the north of Sydney, the site is surrounded by the Ku-ring-gai National Park.

The block extends from the rocky shore past a cliff dominated by an ancient fig tree to the boulder-strewn slope just below the ridgeline. The ridges are characterized by large overhanging sandstone caves.

The house is a series of glass, steel and copper pavilions designed to blend into a stunning natural environment. The lower pavilions are grounded on a massive sandstone retaining wall excavated from the site and engineered to geotechnically stabilize the slope. Arrival involves a boat trip, beach walk and slow hill climb to the enclosing rampart walls of the entry.

The sloping walls lead to the first level bamboo grove with its study, guest bedroom and cellar linked by the huge cantilevering floors of the pavilions above.

The path continues up past the copper-clad walls of the main double-height living pavilion to the original cliff face adorned with the hanging roots of a giant fig tree.

It is here that the fully transparent glass pavilions are revealed and the path continues past the louvered and meshed pantry to the central spine adjoining the kitchen /dining room. This in-between space/verandah links the pavilions and main outdoor deck and disappears when the pavilions are fully opened; it is covered by interlocking layers of steel hoods and copper roofs.

The pavilion form with its large overhangs and warped roof planes privatize the glazed spaces from the neighboring constructions, while also drawing in afternoon light and keeping out the summer sun and rain. Through their small-scale, layout, dark colors and materials, the buildings consciously endeavor to diminish their presence as structures in the National Park.

Steel was selected for its resistance to white ants, bushfires and strength; it has been painted black and designed with a minimum section, while the pavilions are nearly invisible in their structural support.

All material/labor access to the site was by boat or barge to a temporary wharf built over the rocks on the shoreline. Steel or heavy items had to be flown in via helicopter due to the handling difficulties.

The openness of the pavilions captures the shore breezes, while the heat of the sun is screened by hoods. Mechanical metal blinds and large overhangs naturally keep the structures cool in the summer. In the winter, warmth is gained through the open fireplace and radiant heating foils in the ceilings.

The home is particularly sensitive to environmental conditions and responds well to a conservationist ethos. Copper was used extensively for roofs and walls to provide a lasting material with a patina, as it will develop beautifully in this marine environment.

The building collects and stores its own water as well as treating its own waste; it relies on catching the breezes to stay cool and consumes minimal energy for heating.

Photographs: contributed by the architects

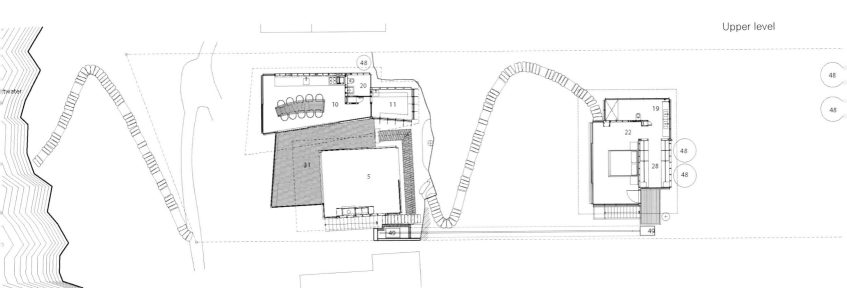

Upper level

48. Water tank
10. Kitchen - dining
11. Pantry
5. Living
22. Master bedroom
28. Dressing room
19. Ensuite
49. Inclinator

Lower level

31. Terrace
25. Bedroom
20. Bathroom
16. Study
12. Cellar
37. Machine room
13. Laundry

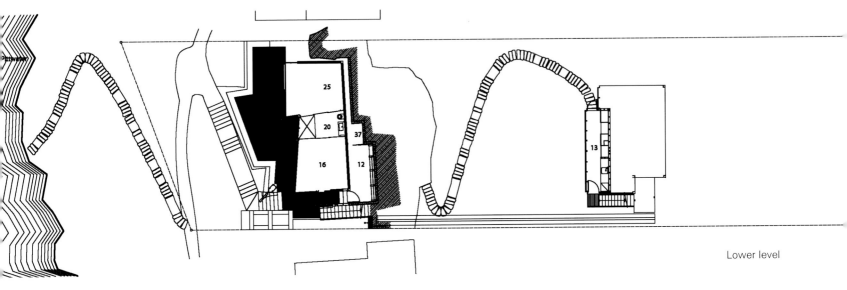

Lower level

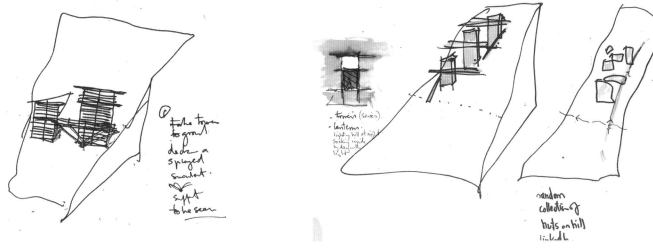

Western elevation - section

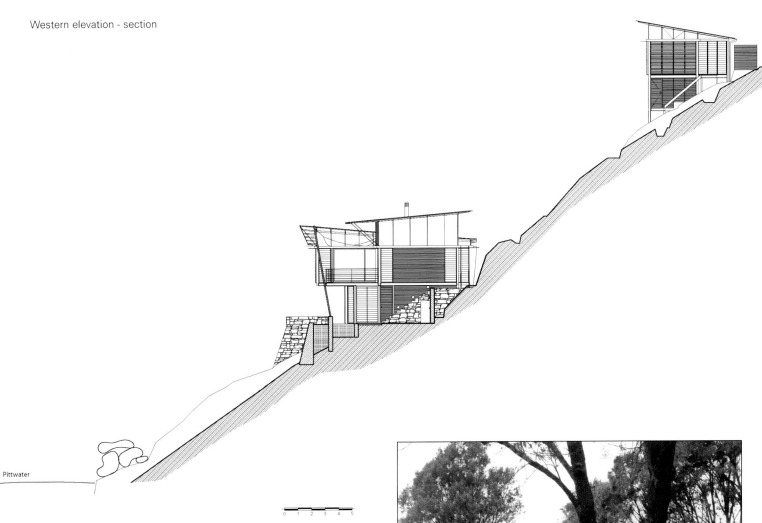

Pittwater

0 1 2 3 4 5

David Chipperfield
House in Galicia

Corrubedo, Galicia, Spain

This house occupies a gap in the main street of the small Galician fishing village of Corrubedo. Sitting at the northern edge of a large protected bay on Spain's northwest Atlantic coast, the site offers dramatic views out over the harbour and to the sea beyond. Unlike the other buildings along the harbour side that turn their backs to the sea, the house looks to exploit the views afforded by its location and orientate all of its internal spaces towards the ocean.

From the sea, the collection of individual and apparently random buildings in Corrubedo form a kind of village elevation - a thin ribbon of buildings that although made up of houses of varying heights and geometries, still presents itself as a unified and solid arrangement.

The introduction of a new house with different priorities had to take into consideration its place within this wall.

Looking to provide a sense of continuity, the house sits on a solid stone and concrete base, and its upper mass, like the neighboring houses, is punctured by small windows. Placed like a shelf between these two conditions, a large panoramic window, extending the full width of the house, provides all encompassing views across the beach and harbor.

Rather than resisting the surrounding geometries, the house takes them into its own form. This strategy is most apparent on the street side of the building where the colliding geometries of adjoining houses extend across the building, dictating its formal composition.

Internally this pattern is repeated with the stairs, bedrooms, and living spaces articulated according to differerent geometries, while on top of the house, introducing its own more organic outline, a large enclosed terrace conforms a protected view of the sea. Looking out from this terrace the house can clearly be seen to maintain a sense of continuity with the rest of the harbor side, while at the same time its silhouette, angular spaces and striking white walls also offer something dramatic, fresh and new.

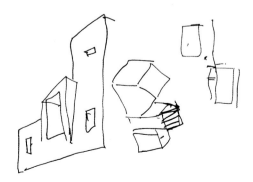

Photographs: Hélène Binet

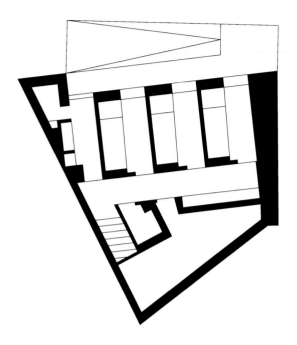

First floor

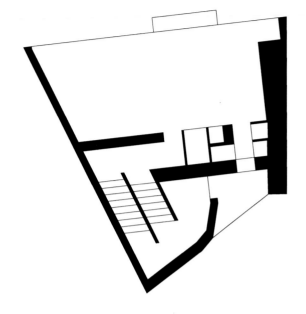

Second floor

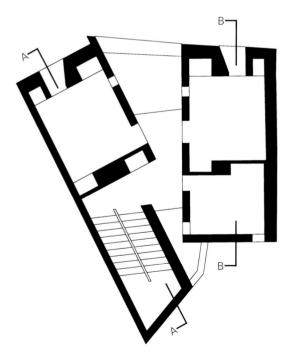

Third floor

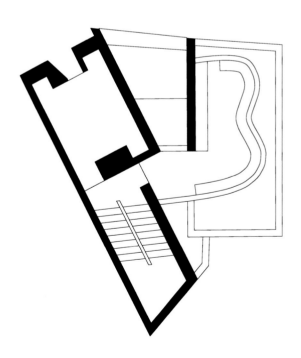

Fourth floor

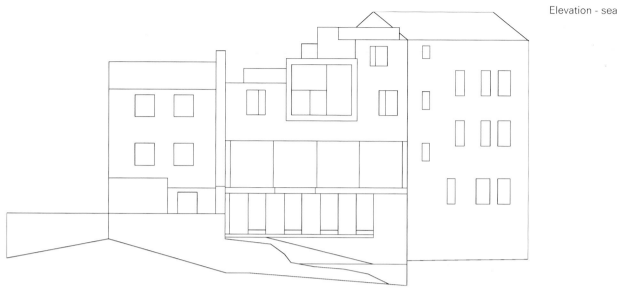

Elevation - sea

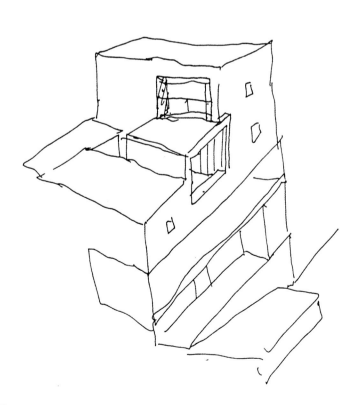

Elevation - street

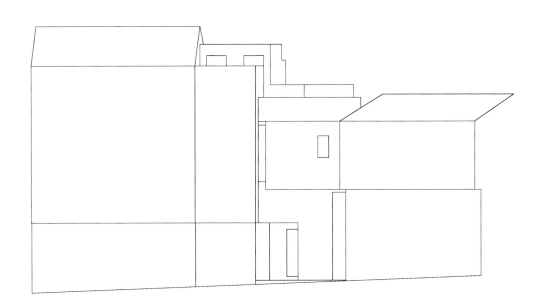

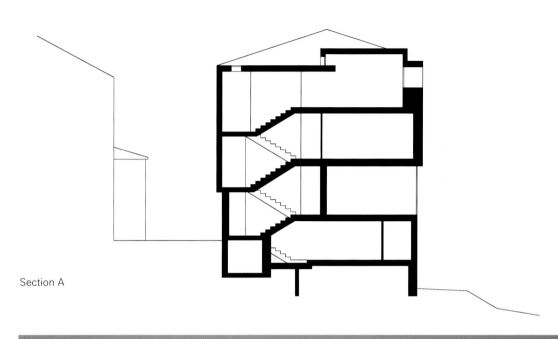

Section A

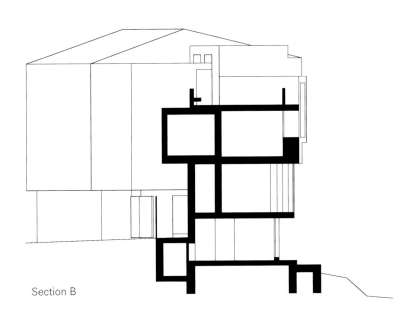

Section B

Jarmund / Vignæs Architects
Villa by the Ocean

Stavanger, Norway

Overlooking the Atlantic Ocean this house is carved into the terrain, allowing an unobstructed ocean view from the public road at the rear and protecting the building from the winds.

The bedrooms have been strategically laid out to face the naturally sheltered outdoor spaces, thus gaining close-up views as well. At the same time, the living room is established as a glazed amphitheater facing the horizon. The walls are made of two-sided white concrete cast in situ.

In general, the materials used are related to site conditions. White sand from the beach is used in the concrete, the roofs are covered with turf and pebbles from a nearby river.

Inside, the concrete surfaces are mainly kept untreated except for parts which are clad in whitewashed oak, lined with aluminum and covered with sisal carpeting or turquoise tiles.

The aluminum of the flashing and window frames diffuses the sunlight like the sea mist.

Photographs: Nils Petter Dale

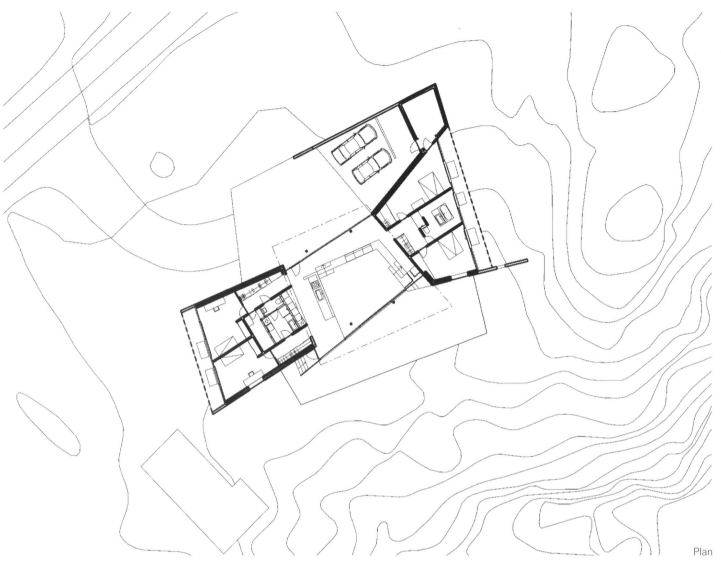

Plan

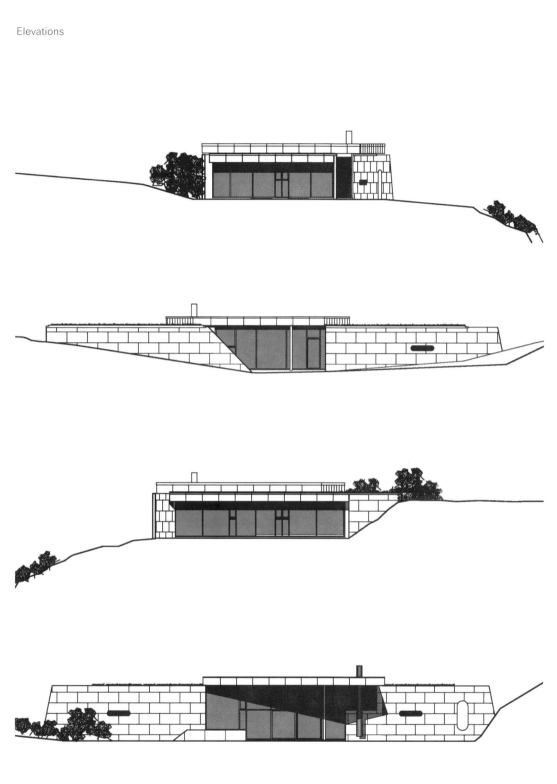

Jaime Sanahuja
Single-Family House

Oropesa, Spain

The house, a summer and weekend retreat for a large family, sits on one of the hills of a recently developed area and enjoys magnificent views of the sea and an optimal southeast orientation, which played a central role in the implantation of the building on the site.

The project organizes all of the exterior spaces, making use of the site's very pronounced slope. At the lower end is a large basement/parking garage, which features both a closed in, private area and another more public zone from which the main entryway opens into the habitable spaces. Here, also, are the service staff's rooms and the technical installations.

The rest of the parcel has been terraced into various horizontal platforms that rise toward the main house, where the primary terrace is set between the dwelling and the swimming pool, which serves as a horizon over the sea. This area enjoys cool sea breezes and excellent views.

The program for the home required its development practically on a single level, while the ground floor houses the guest rooms and a studio. The latter, on one hand, creates a rich, double-height interior space above the living room and, on the other, helps configure the exterior volumetrics, being laid out with respect to the units into which the main floor has been fragmented.

The simplification of the use of materials and colors – Capri marble, white rendering coat on the exterior and white walls inside – unifies the perception of the program as a whole, placing emphasis on the horizontal planes of the terraces and balconies as well as on the large glazed surfaces, which enhance indoor-outdoor connections and show off the magnificent panorama.

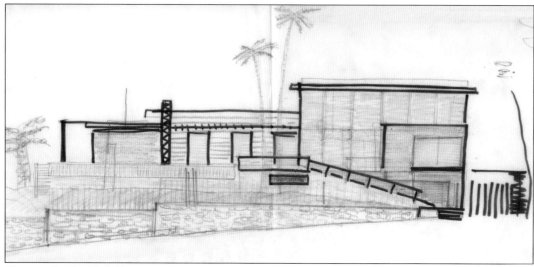

Photographs: José Luis Hausmann

Basement

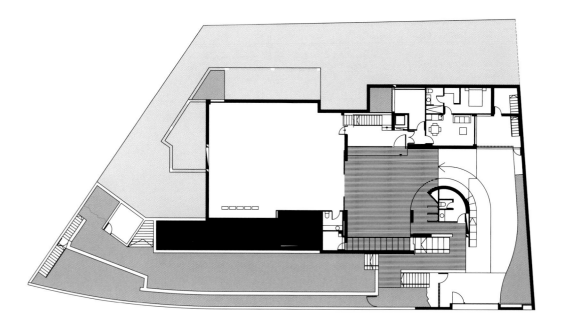

First floor

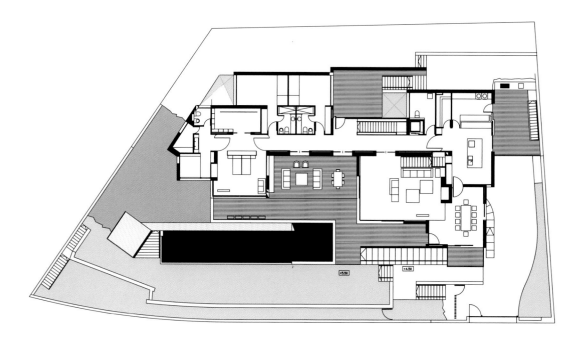

North elevation

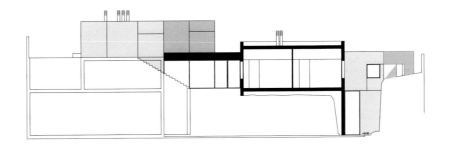

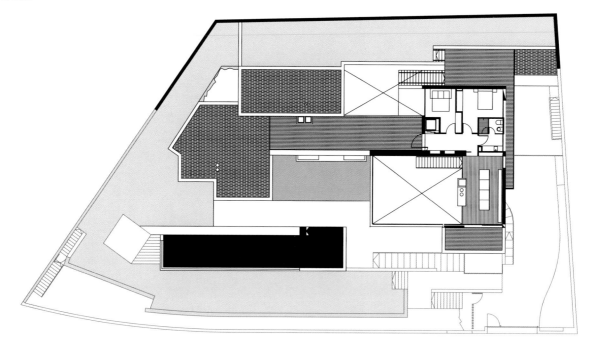

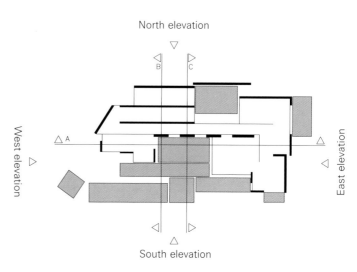

North elevation

West elevation

East elevation

South elevation

B C

A

South elevation

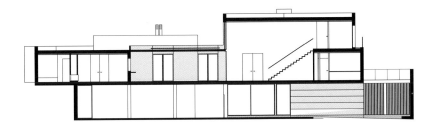

Section A

Due to its privileged orientation towards the best views, the floor plan was an attempt to resolve the articulation and transition zones between the bedrooms and living areas, as well as between the entrance and the terraces, with a sense of spaciousness and elegance.

East elevation

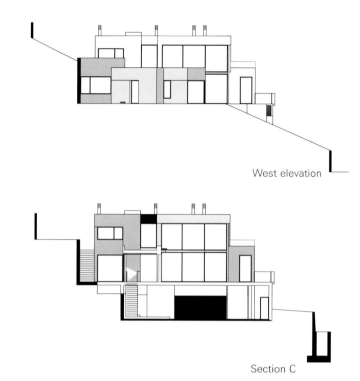

West elevation

Section B

Section C

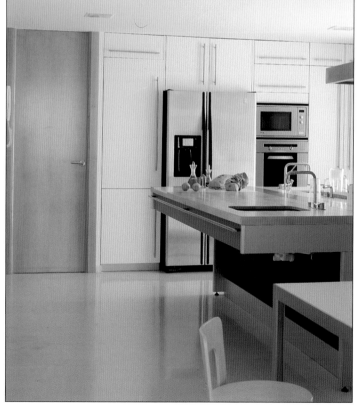

Taken as a whole, the house and its various terraces create a new artificial topography on the hill into which they have been implanted.

Chiba Manabu Architects
Kashima Surf Villa

Kashima, Japan

Located just meters from a long stretch of sandy beach, effectively separating land and water, Kashima Surf Villa possesses an architecture of dialect between private and public spaces and functions, all in harmony with the existing "natural" tension between the ocean and the beach.

Conceived as a shared, corporate villa for a group of friends, where both intimacy and communal gathering imposed their own sets of requirements, the architect succeeded in creating two pairs of connected, yet separate, spatial entities.

On one hand, two box-like shapes define the private space of the 9 bedrooms, grouping 5 north-facing rooms on the first floor, and another 4 south-facing rooms in the upper box. In each box, the color of the interior walls counterbalances the effect of natural light: with white in the rooms facing the north and black in those facing the south, a light equilibrium is consequently created.

On the other hand, the consequence of creating these two "diagonally positioned" boxes is that the "negative space" creates another diagonal direction, visually tying a pair of shared/public spaces, the 1st floor to the 2nd floor.

Remarkably, standard notions of 1st and 2nd floor divisions disappear here, giving a new dimension to the perception of levels inside the house: the 2nd floor is immediately felt here as being the roof of the first box. From the first floor, one climbs a stairway leading to this "inner roof", accentuated by the use of the wooden parquet as flooring. To highlight more this roof/floor effect, the 2nd box of bedrooms is positioned higher than the 2nd floor, standing independently from the rest of the space, and creating a third floor.

It is because of this leveling method that an exciting small space was created, sandwiched in between these two surfaces: behind the top of the stairway, a low-height space forces the dweller to sit on the floor, as in a tea room, contemplating the ocean in the horizon.

Although this dialect of two intertwining spaces has appeared in some of the architect's previous residential designs, the spatial gap in Kashima Surf Villa between the two poles is obviously wider.

Photographs: Nácàsa & Partners

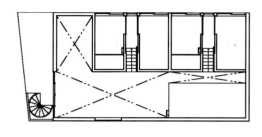

Second floor

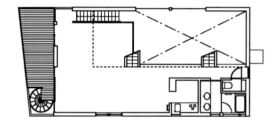

First floor

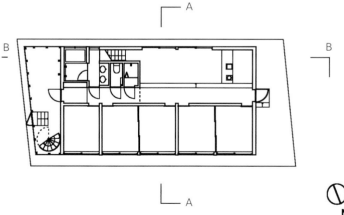

Ground floor

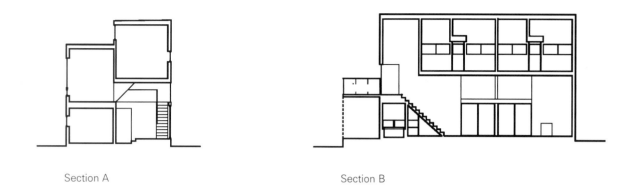

Section A   Section B

Carlos Ferrater - Joan Guibernau
Tagomago House

Ibiza, Spain

The house is located on a slightly sloped plot in the northeast part of the Island of Ibiza, to the north of the city of Santa Eulalia, in a wild Mediterranean landscape facing the sea and the Island of Tagomago.

Due to its use as a vacation house, the final layout made the dwelling the central nucleus around which other dependant pieces and small autonomous pavilions were arranged. This enables a progressive and flexible use that varies according to the number of inhabitants. The articulation of the home via a lengthwise axis provides for perfectly orientated isolated pieces that may be entirely independent.

The program grew in the manner of rural constructions, by the addition of different components and rooms, giving great importance to the spatial and environmental connections between these white stone volumes facing the sea and bathed in Mediterranean light. The complex thus achieves an ambience reminiscent of Arabian and southern Mediterranean architecture, while at the same time providing a relaxed, serene climate not unlike a monastic construction. The use of two pure, untreated materials also contributes to this atmosphere: bare white stone and white concrete cast in situ. The absence of landscaped elements, instead conserving or restoring the natural terrain around the building, enhances the subliminal image of the work.

The program allows for functional flexibility and the use of such traditional construction elements as concrete, stone and wood.

The living room opens onto a large wooden terrace that serves as an open-air communal meeting place. A sizable reinforced concrete, porch-like canopy (in white to match the stone) set alongside the swimming pool forms part of this outdoor space.

Abutting the main rooms are four smaller pavilions for the children; these have been designed to adapt to future changes and eventual additional family members. Finally, a terrace/solarium sits above a guest-room.

In spite of the use of traditional materials, the construction system is completely contemporary, as seen in the use of an interior load-bearing wall, which is composed of an outer shell of waterproofed concrete around an air chamber and insulation material. This is clad in an outer skin of self-supporting traditional stone blocks measuring 15x40x80 cm which are affixed to the wall with stainless steel bands. Likewise, the stone, being highly porous, has been treated to keep water out.

Photographs: Alejo Bagué

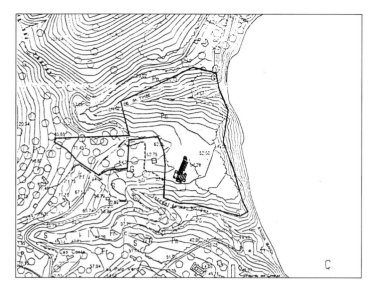

The organization of the home's spaces, composed of autonomous, isolated pieces, enabled the creation of a series of open areas, patios, porches and terraces, all of which serves to establish imprecise boundaries between interior and exterior.

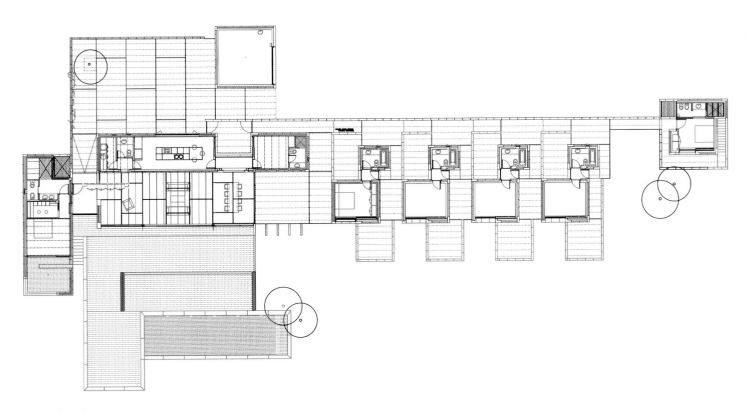

Plan and sections

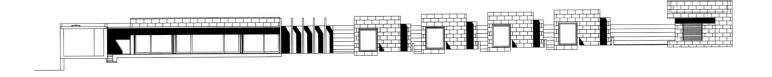

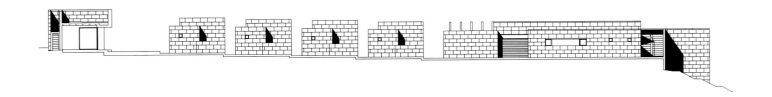

The construction systems have been simplified as much as possible. Few materials were used and, whenever possible, these were obtained from the islands: stone walls and facades, traditional slabs using concrete beams and ceramic vaults, wood carpentry and exterior paving in stone, concrete and wood.

KHR AS Arkitekter

Guesthouse at Nissum Bredning

Jutland, Denmark

In the late 1930's, painter Jens Søndergaard moved into a house in Toftum, and in a letter to his friend, Leo Svane he described "landscapes so wonderfully expansive they were beyond comparison with Thy".

The artist's fascination with the special light, the strong sweeping Toftum Bjerge hills and the Limfjord region's wide open skies inspired a number of distinctive paintings, often done in the same area where the guest house was built. The house is built into a hilly slope, with a 200 degree panorama view from east to west over an open, un-built dune and meadow area running down toward the Nissum Bredning coast.

One of the goals was to capture the light from the sky in a continuous spatial sequence in one building, which, when seen from any direction, respects the profile of the hill ridge. The guest area consists of two parts, a concrete slab cov-ered with basalt, and a copper shell. The slab serves as the floor, a continuous plane running from the morning terrace in the east to the evening terrace in the west. The shell serves as both facade and roof and is closed toward the slope to the south and open toward the north.

The roof is punctured by a continuous skylight, which spatially separates the secondary functions in the closed core toward the south from the primary functions in the more open spatial sequence in the other three directions.

The bearing construction consists of steel frames, while the roof and outer walls consist of prefabricated wooden coffers dimensioned according to the building's primary grid.

The exterior copper siding is a rare sight in Denmark; felt with a thin, flexible copper covering, with a textured, waffled surface due to the compression of the copper and felt.

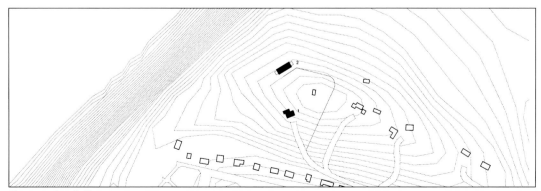

Photographs: Ib Sorensen

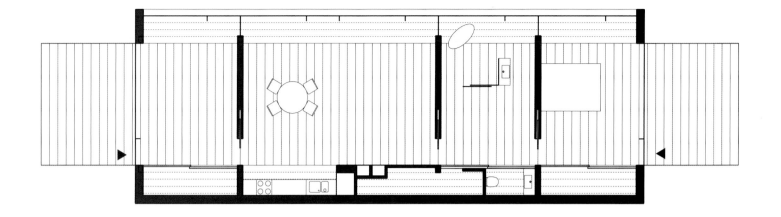

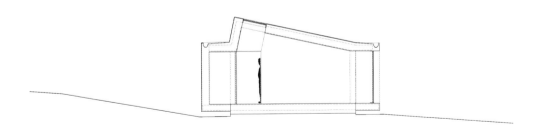

Biselli + Katchborian

Guaecá Beach House

São Sebastião, Brazil

The site is located on Guaecá Beach, São Sebastião, on the north coast of the State of São Paulo, and is surrounded by the mountains of Serra do Mar and the almost overwhelming green of the Mata Atlântica rain forest.

In accordance with local conservation laws, sixty percent of the existing trees on the site were left in place.

The program called for a five-bedroom house with dining, TV and living rooms, a kitchen barbecue and service areas, all of which has been distributed throughout two floors. In addition, there is a partially underground floor for the garage and a sauna/bathroom.

The upper floor houses four bedrooms and the TV room, while the areas destined for entertaining and gathering, as well as an additional bedroom for guests, are on the ground floor.

The south and east perimeters of the house are skirted by ample terraces and verandas leading directly to the edge of the swimming pool, which has been designed in an L-shape to hug this corner of the house. The wooden verandahs are entirely open and have no railings, leaving an unimpeded path for diving straight into the pool. The construction techniques primarily made use of cast concrete and masonry. The terraces are made with steel frames topped by dark wood decks. The roof features a traditional wooden structure with metal shingles.

Photographs: Nelson Kon

Ground floor plan

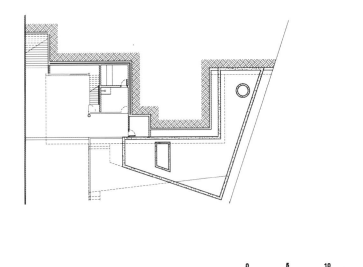

0   5   10

First floor plan

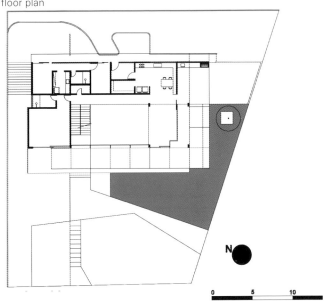

N

0   5   10

Second floor plan

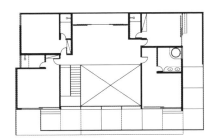

147

South-east elevation

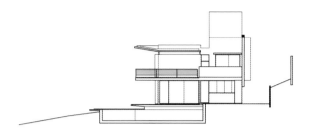

South-west elevation

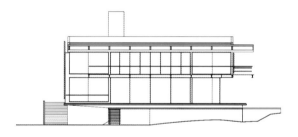

North-west elevation

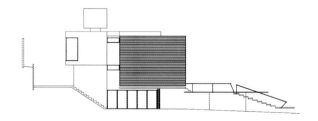

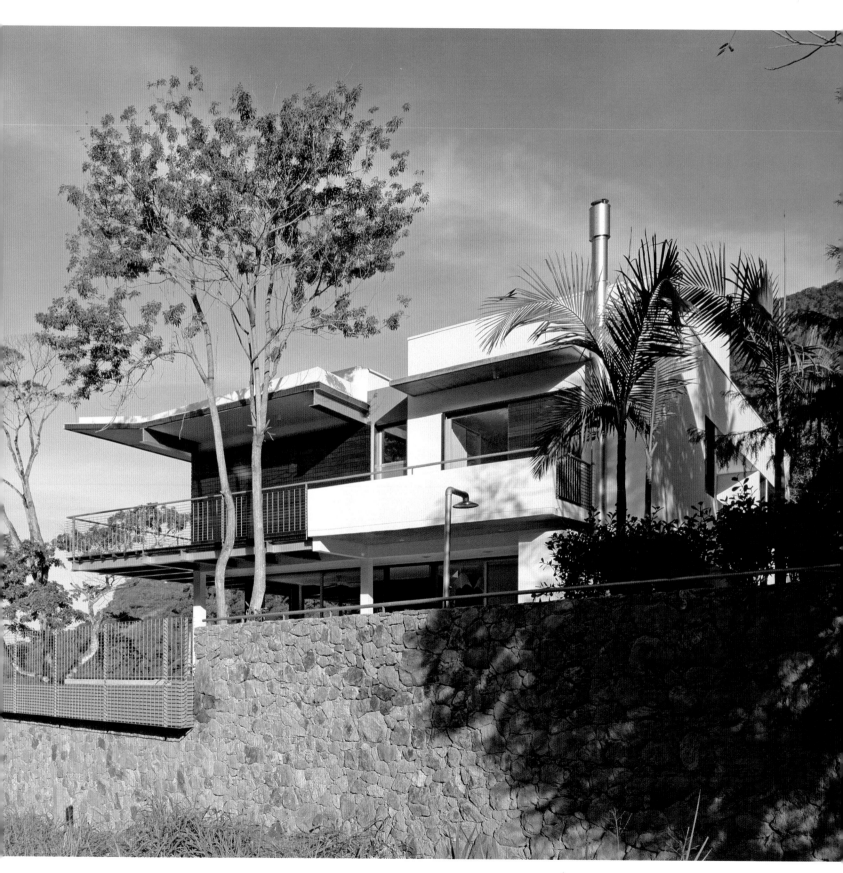

Longitudinal section

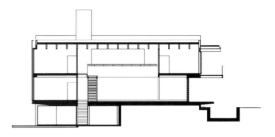

Cross section

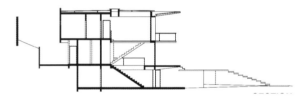

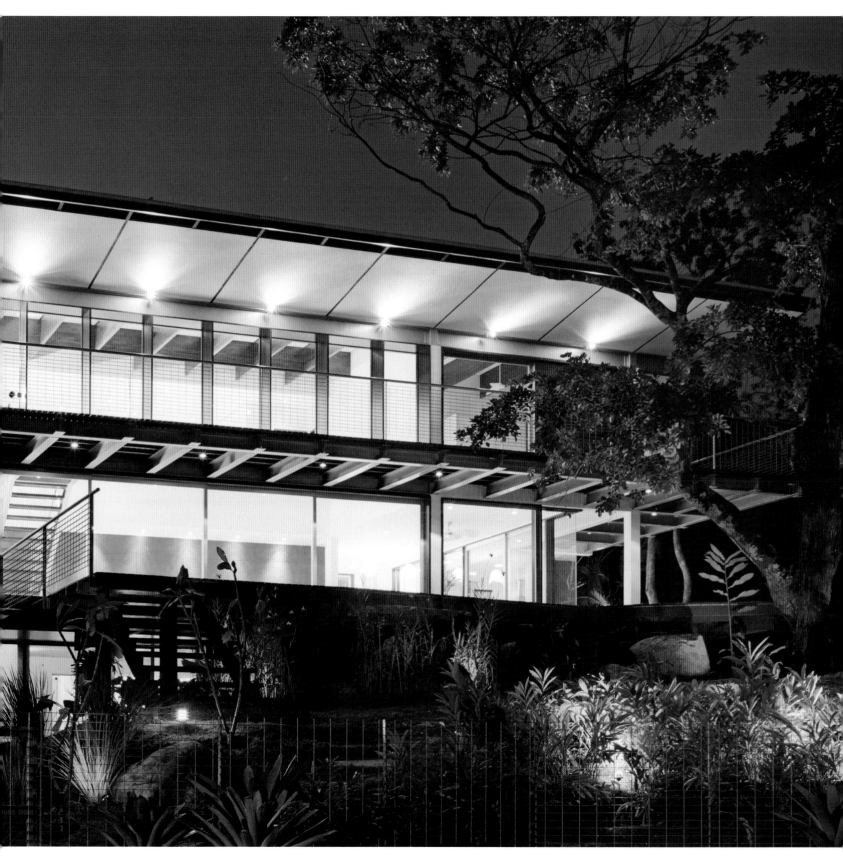

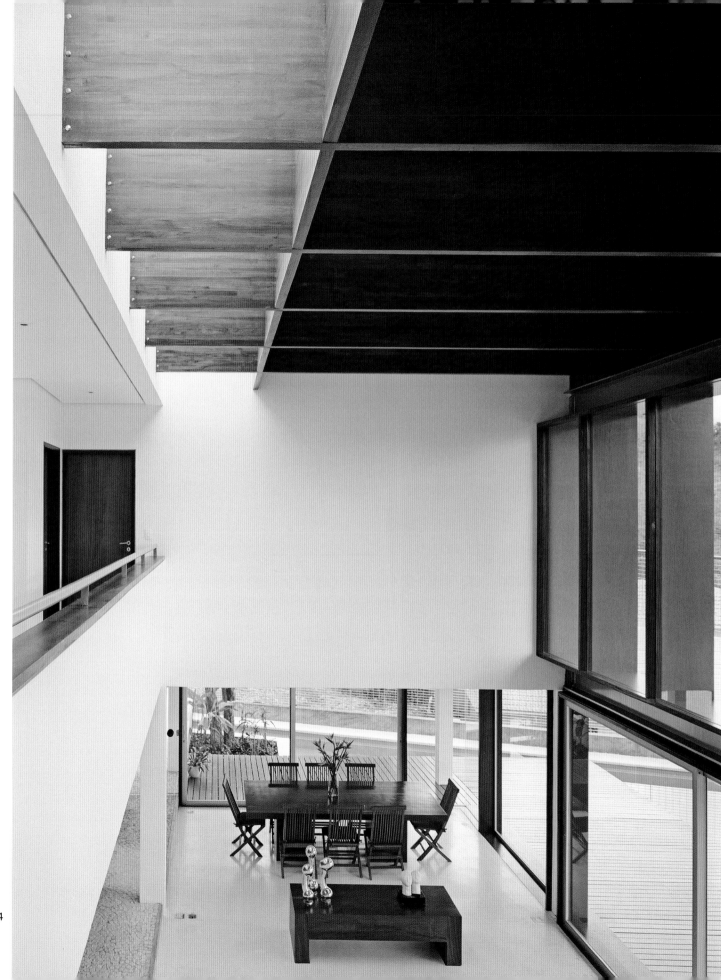

Christophe Bidaud Architecte
Boutin House

Puys, France

The concept guiding the program was based on the study of two important factors. First was the family's present and projected lifestyle and, secondly, were the concrete topographical conditions presented by the site.

The house is laid out on two levels with the necessary articulations to ensure comfortable cohabitation of parents and children. Furthermore, the areas for day use are clearly distinct from the bedrooms, with a kitchen/dining room/living room continuing toward the terrace comprising the axis of the family's daily life and social gatherings.

To the rather strict spatial distribution are added numerous wide openings, framing the sea in the distance and bringing in the maximum amount of natural light.

One of the central tenets of the design was that it should respect the land as far as possible. To achieve this end, and create a harmoniously interacting program, the house has been conceived as a sort of pier, being erected on concrete pillars with a diameter of 20 centimeters. This structure resting on pillars allowed the architects to do away with the standard ground floor anchored to the earth, a style that would have too closely emulated that of the neighboring buildings. At the same time it considerably lightens the impact of the construction on the relatively wild terrain. On the other hand, this solution evokes seaside structures and will also provide a shaded space for parking cars.

The choice of materials fits in well with the volumetric concept: wood, with its seeming lightness, enables an air of levity free from the structural limitations ordinarily imposed by traditional brick constructions.

The dynamic nature of the design is further enhanced by the combination of wide eaves, a stepped profile, opposing forms (a cylinder and parallelepiped, for example) and the organic rhythm of the wood grain, all of which comes together to visually lighten the exterior.

Finally, the projected landscaping scheme has been kept to a minimum of intervention: all of the existing trees but one will be conserved. The small open spaces will follow the style of an English garden and a gravel pathway will lead from the parking area to the entryway.

Photographs: MC Bordaz

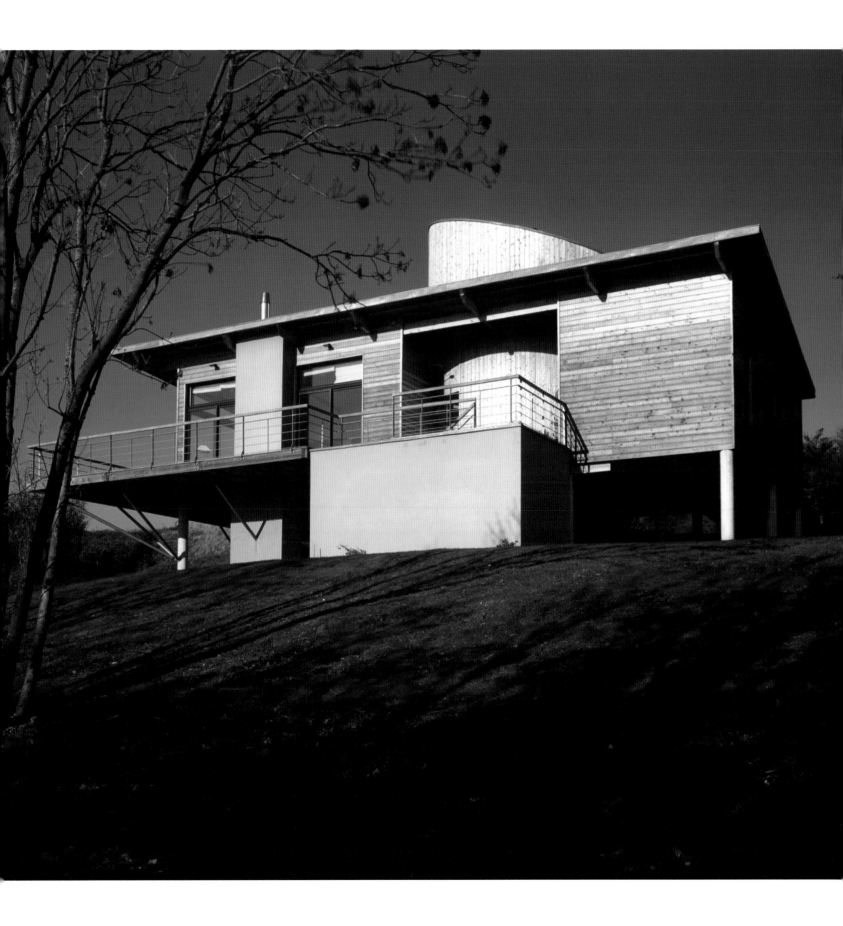

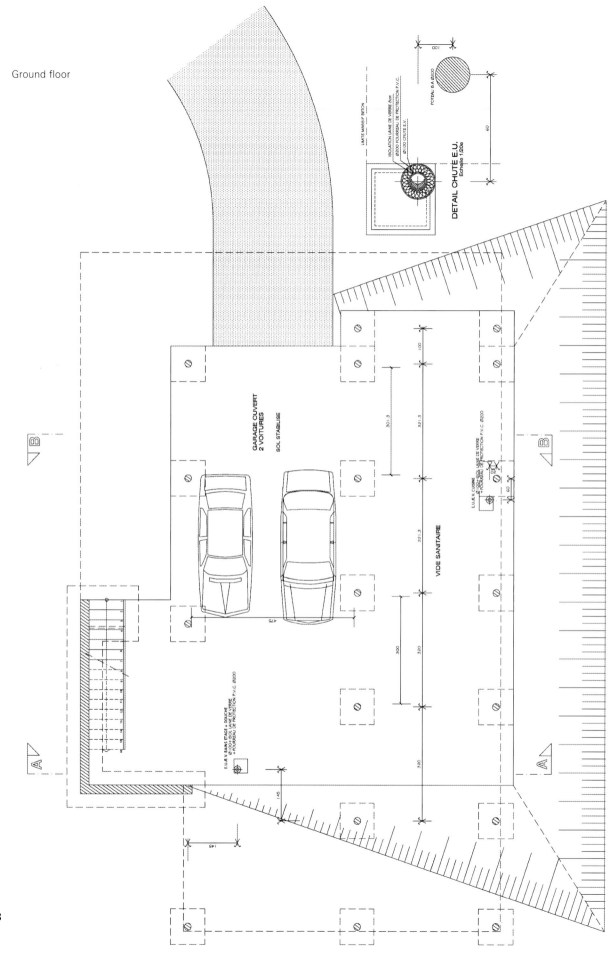

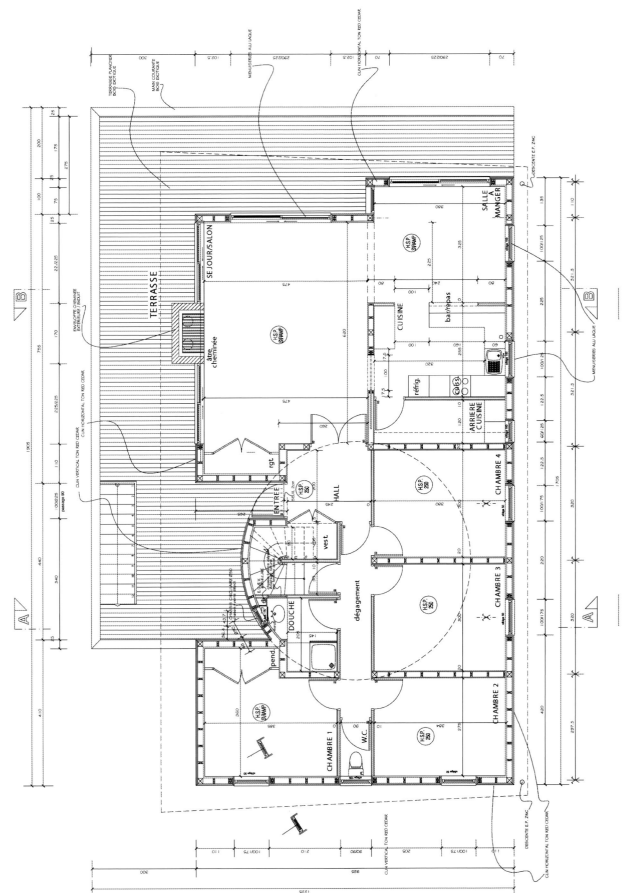

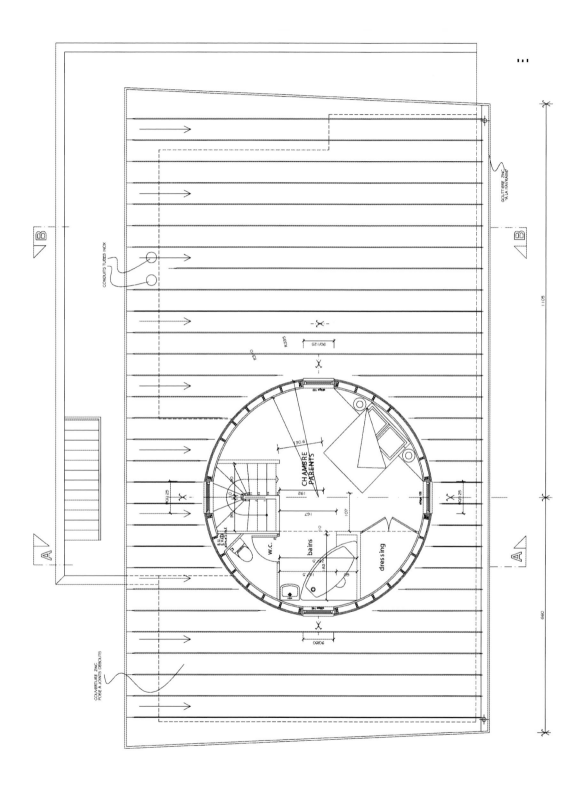

Section B

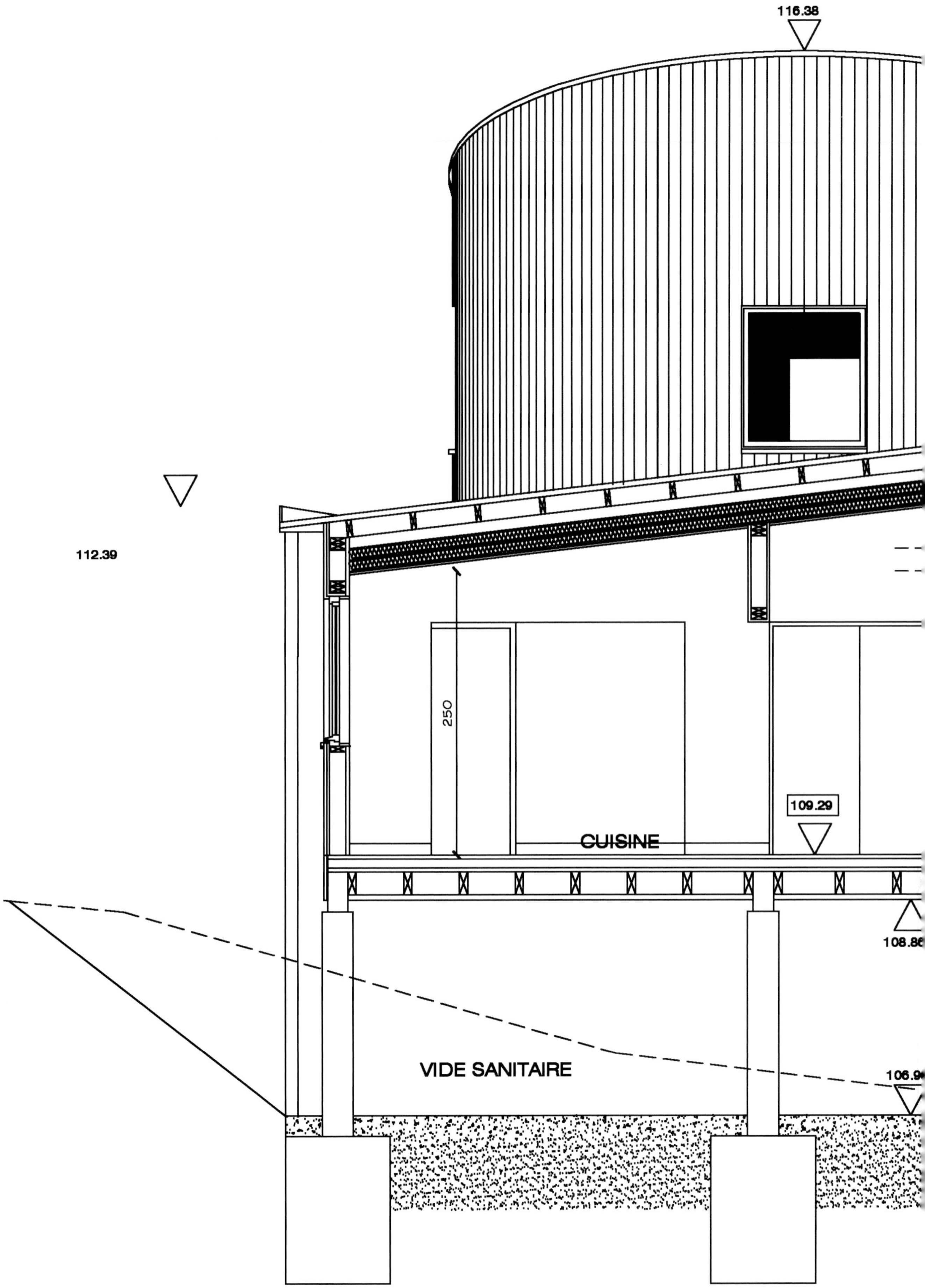
116.38
112.39
250
109.29
CUISINE
108.86
VIDE SANITAIRE
106.9

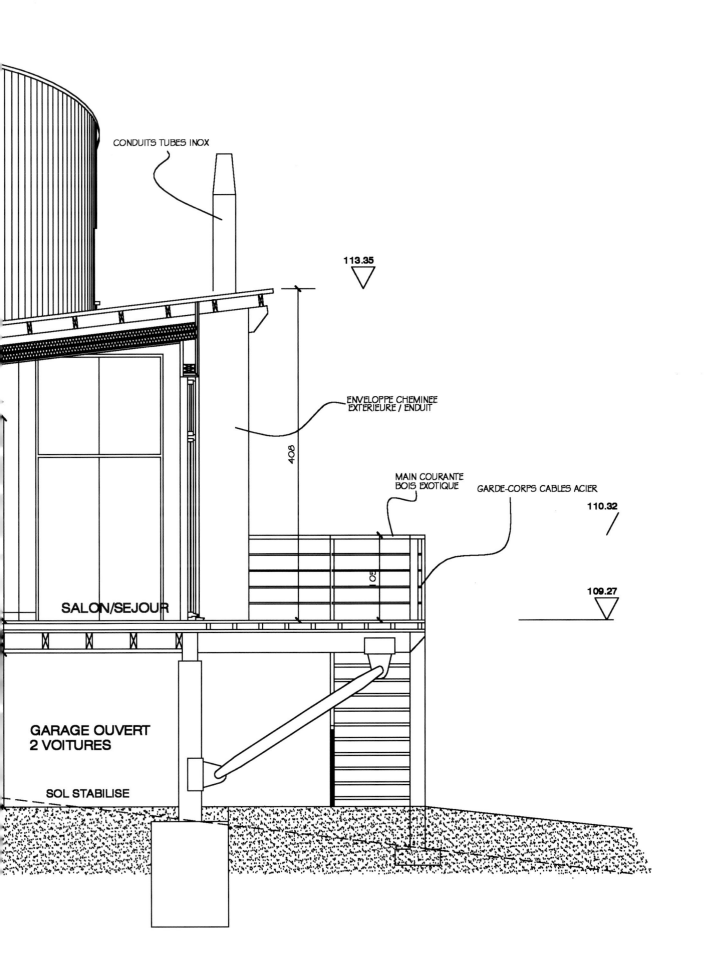

CONDUITS TUBES INOX

113.35 ▽

ENVELOPPE CHEMINEE
EXTERIEURE / ENDUIT

4.08

MAIN COURANTE
BOIS EXOTIQUE

GARDE-CORPS CABLES ACIER

110.32

109.27 ▽

SALON/SEJOUR

GARAGE OUVERT
2 VOITURES

SOL STABILISE

163

167

Christoff Finio
Beach House

Long Beach Island, New Jersey, USA

A barrier island off the southern coast of New Jersey, Long Beach Island has developed into both a year-round and a seasonal community. The project sits on the ocean side of the island, within the contours of a thickly wooded dune that stretches several hundred yards to the Atlantic Ocean. While there are properties developed on both the immediate north and west, they are barely apparent, due to the careful siting of the house, the design of its envelope, and the programming of its interior.

The property consists of three combined lots, totaling approximately 150' square. However, over half of the property is considered protected wetlands by the DEP, and as such could not be built upon. The house hugs much of the line delineating these protected wetlands, while complying with all minimum setback requirements from adjacent properties. All occupiable spaces must be a minimum of eleven feet above sea level, and the house may not exceed 35 feet in height, as measured from the crown of the adjacent road.

The clients are a couple with two young children from the Philadelphia area who have spent their summers on the island for the past ten years. They were drawn to this particular property for its uniquely wooded and secluded character; a site that amounts to a secret in the open. The many trees are a result of the previous landown-er's weekend plantings over the course of some twenty years, and the clients maintained a strong desire to always feel among these trees while inside the main living area. This led to the idea of lifting the main functions of the house above the ground and entering underneath them, so that living occurs at the level of the tree canopy, and the more private functions of the house occur above the trees with a view to the ocean. A guest bedroom, an office/gym and a storage room form the three points of support that elevate the main house, which in turn forms the covered exterior space and breezeway at grade level.

The program includes kitchen, living/dining room, outdoor room, office/gym, five bedrooms, five bathrooms, three outdoor showers and a pool house with lap pool and Jacuzzi. The total interior space is 4,100 square feet, and the total amount of exterior deck is 4,900 square feet.

Wood piles and concrete pile caps comprise the foundation. The structural frame is a hybrid of steel and engineered wood. Walls are wood frame and plywood. Exterior sheathing is Western Red Cedar shiplap siding. Interior walls are skim coat plaster over wallboard. The roof is fiberglass reinforced resin over plywood, with a lead-coated copper coping. Windows and exterior decking are mahogany.

Photographs: Elizabeth Felicella

A ridge of tall, thickly wooded dunes separates this house from the ocean, some 200 yards away. Responding to the limited allowable buildable area of the site, the house is conceived as a dense grouping of volumes, stacked in such a way to allow for enclosed outdoor spaces, both expansive and intimate, and loft-like interior spaces which look out over the tops of the trees to the shore.

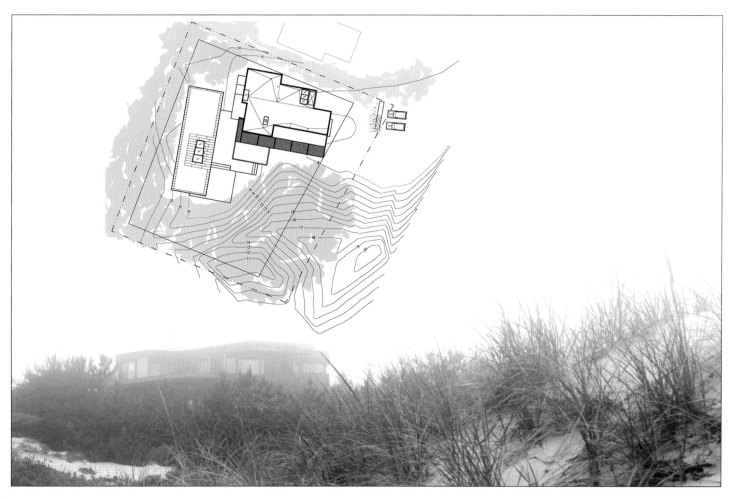

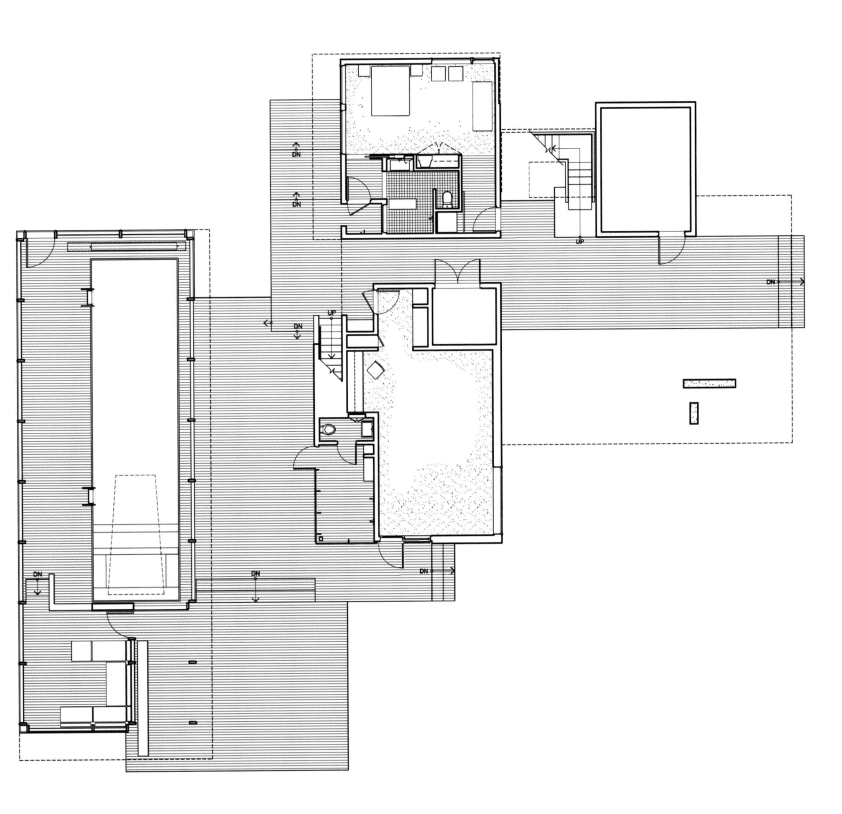

First floor plan

A

B

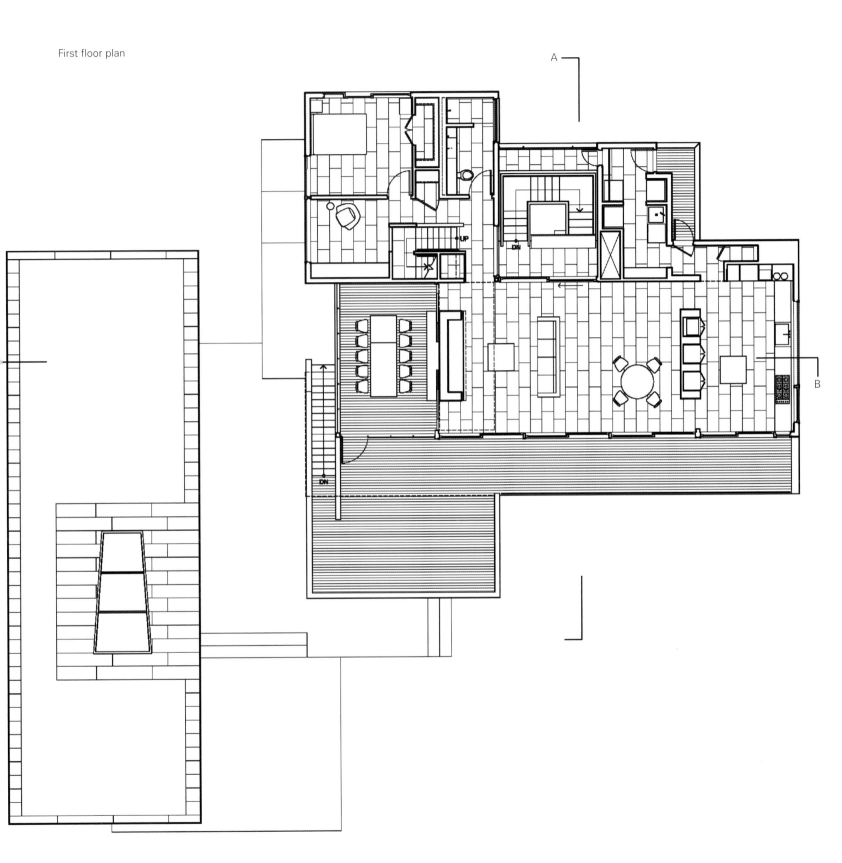

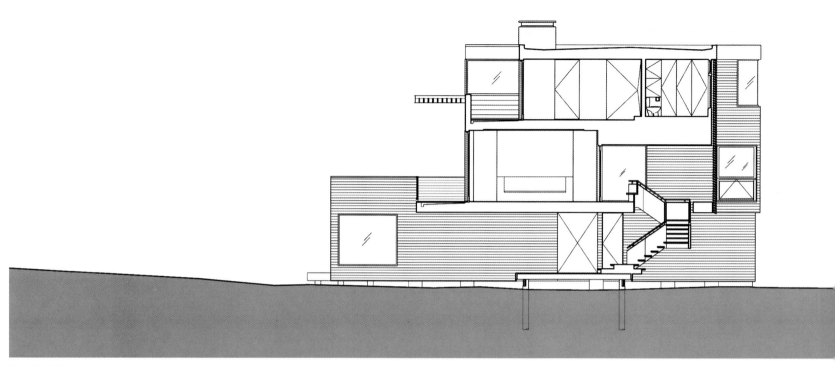

Secction A

Section B

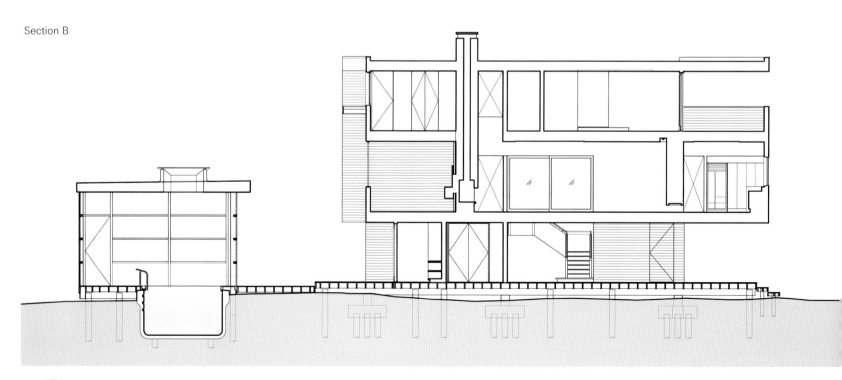

174

Wall section at guest bedroom

1. Fiberglass roof over ¾" exterior grade plywood slope to drain
2. Lead coated copper parapet (typical)
3. Hurricane clips at each joist (typical)
4. 1 x 10 rabbeted cedar fascia
5. Cedar soffit over ¾" exterior grade plywood
6. Veneer plaster sheetrock
7. Insulation: R30 Kraft face, fiberglass batts
8. 12" Shiplap cedar siding recessed between windows
9. Insulation: R19 Kraft face, fiberglass batts
10. 3" T&G ebonized oak flooring
11. Lead coated copper flashing
12. 3" furr-out over recessed shear wall with 4" Shiplap cedar siding
13. 2 ½ Fry reglet reveal base
14. 5 ¼x117/8" P.L.
15. Veneer plaster sheetrock
16. 2 x 6 shear wall beyond
17. 2 x 6 shear wall with 4" Shiplap cedar siding
18. ¾" Stone floor over 1" setting bed and ¾" plywood subfloor
19. Insulation: R22 Kraft face, fiberglass batts
20. 2 ½ Fry reglet reveal base
21. Steel structure
22. Vapor barrier
23. Exterior grade plywood
24. T&G Cedar soffit over ½" exterior grade plywood
25. Veneer plaster sheetrock over ½" plywood
26. 2x6 shear wall with ½" plywood each side
27. 4" Shiplap cedar siding
28. Vapor barrier
29. ½" exterior grade plywood
30. Insulation: R19 Kraft face, fiberglass batts
31. ½" plywood
32. Veneer plaster sheetrock
33. Carpet & underlayment
34. ¾" plywood
35. Insulation: R22 Kraft face, fiberglass batts
36. Hurricane clips at each joist (typical)
37. (2) 3x12' s (typical)
38. 12" typical pile

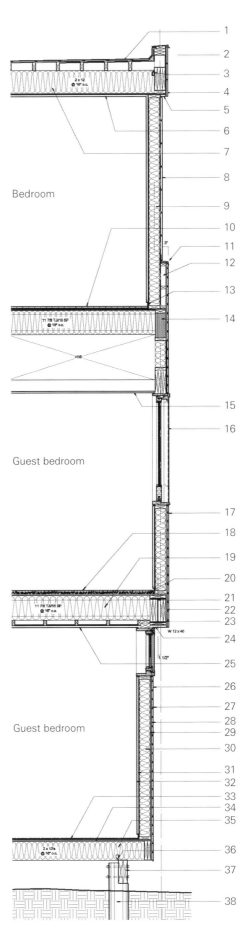

Bedroom

Guest bedroom

Guest bedroom

177

Wood screens are used to connect spaces, modulate light and privacy, and, in the case of the pool house, to provide the most reductive sense of enclosure. Stone, wood, and glass form a limited palette, detailed to avoid distraction.

Crosson Clarke Carnachan Architects

Coromandel Bach

Coromandel, New Zealand

This mid-sized house (with 128 sqm of floor space) was conceived as a container sitting lightly on the land for habitation or the dream of habitation. The intention was to reinterpret the New Zealand building tradition of the crafting of wood - the expression of structure, cladding, lining and joinery in a raw and unique way. The construction is reminiscent of the 'trip' or 'rafter' dams common in the Coromandel region at the turn of last century: heavy vertical structural members supporting horizontal boarding.

The unadorned natural timber, a sustainable and renewable resource, provides a connection to nature and the natural. A simple mechanism to the deck allows the 'box' to open up on arrival, providing a stage for living, and to close down on departure, providing protection.

The house has a simple rectangular plan that sits across the contour in a patch of cleared bush in the manner of the rural shed, facing north and enjoying unobstructed views.

The living room is open to the outside and the sun, a metaphorical tent or campsite, while the bunkrooms are enclosed and cool. The large fireplace allows winter occupation and the open bathroom and moveable bath allows the rituals of showering and bathing to become an experience connected to nature.

This 'bach' is an attempt to provide an environment to capture the essential spirit of a New Zealand vacation home set in the scenic New Zealand landscape. ('Bach' is a typical New Zealand word that describes a weekend cottage or house, usually at the beach).

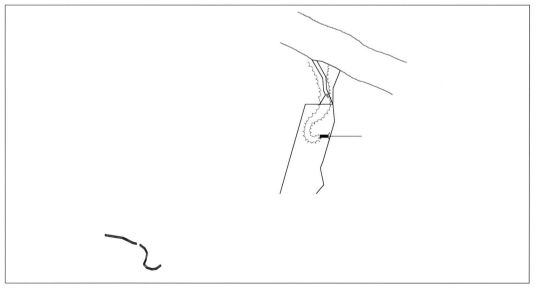

Photographs: Patrick Reynolds

Plan

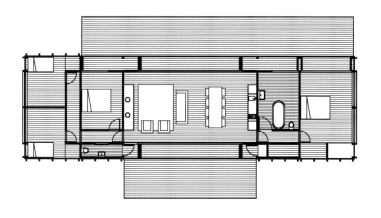

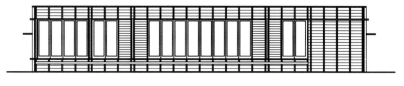

North elevation

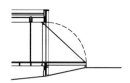

Section - Deck lowered

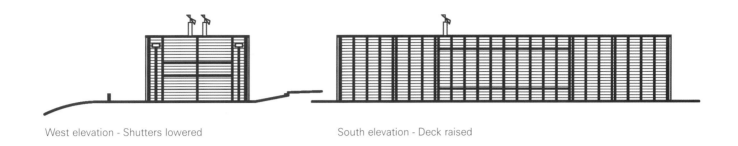

West elevation - Shutters lowered   South elevation - Deck raised

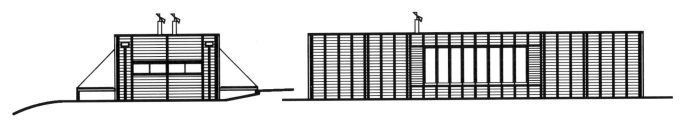

West elevation - Shutters raised

South elevation - Deck lowered

Cross-section

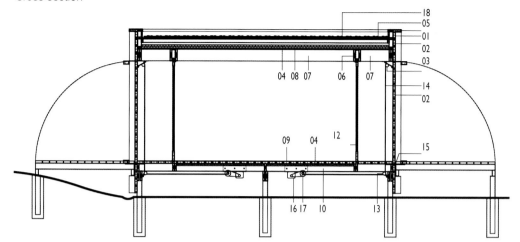

01. Flashing
02. Lawson Cyprus cladding/decking
03. Building wrap
04. Insulation
05. Membrane roof over plywood
06. Steel beam / lintel
07. Exposed Lawson Cyprus rafters
08. Plywood ceiling
09. Timber flooring
10. Timber joists
11. Timber piles / bearers
12. Bi-fold doors
13. Single block
14. Spectra rope
15. 20mm Stainless steel hinge
16. Electric motor
17. Axle
18. River stones

The living room is open to the outside and the sun, like a tent or campsite. The open bathroom and moveable bath allows the rituals of showering and bathing to become an experience connected to nature.

Enric Sòria
House in Port d´Addaia

Port d´Addaia, Menorca, Spain

The home sits on a parcel in a rather ordinary urbanized zone on the Menorcan coast, while at the same time enjoying a privileged location directly overlooking the sea and a small natural port, Port d'Addaia, in the northern part of the island. The backdrop to the spectacular views is the pristine coastline of the land on the opposite side of the port.

The parcel of land measures 670 sqm and is affected by local norms protecting the coastline. Furthermore, the land slopes sharply toward the sea, necessitating a terracing of the site. With a total surface area of 226 sqm and a slightly trapezoidal floor plan measuring 109 sqm, the dwelling is a very simple prismatic volume. One very open side faces the east and the sea, while the west-facing façade has received particular attention in its surface treatment; the two side walls are almost entirely blind.

The room distribution spans three levels, the uppermost featuring the entryway and living room and being set just slightly below the level of the access road. A second level, set just below the first, includes the bedrooms and bathrooms, while the lowermost level opens out onto a porch sitting alongside the open space of the yard and swimming pool area. The two top levels are joined via an interior stairwell, while the lower porch is accessed from the exterior.

The main east-facing façade is presided over by a spacious terrace, which is an extraordinary lookout point from which to take in the natural scenery of the port. This terrace occupies the entire width of the façade and is connected directly to the dining room, living room and kitchen via a wide expanse of floor-to-ceiling sliding glass doors. Beneath this level, the bedrooms enjoy access to smaller, individual balconies of nearly a meter in depth, with an exterior enclosure of adjustable slats, which effectively create a cool, enclosed chamber to mitigate the intensity of the Mediterranean light.

The lower porch opens outward toward a small swimming pool that overlooks the sea. On the other side of the house, a line of shrubbery set parallel to the road and running the width of the house ensures privacy. Here also is a small guest apartment.

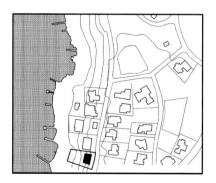

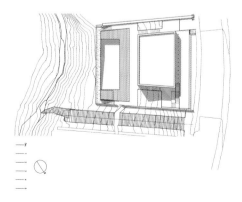

Photographs: Lluís Casals

Upper floor

Lower floor

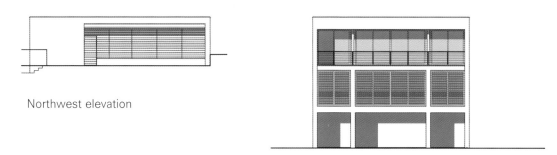

Northwest elevation

Southeast elevation

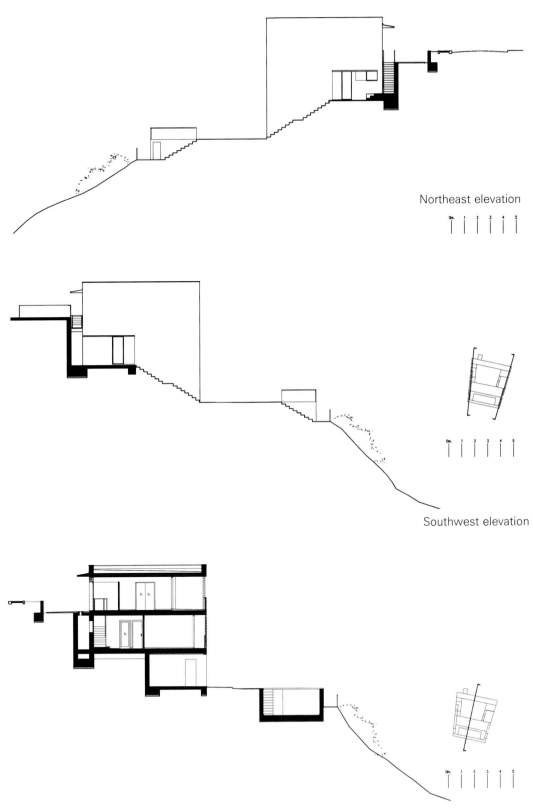

Northeast elevation

Southwest elevation

Cross section

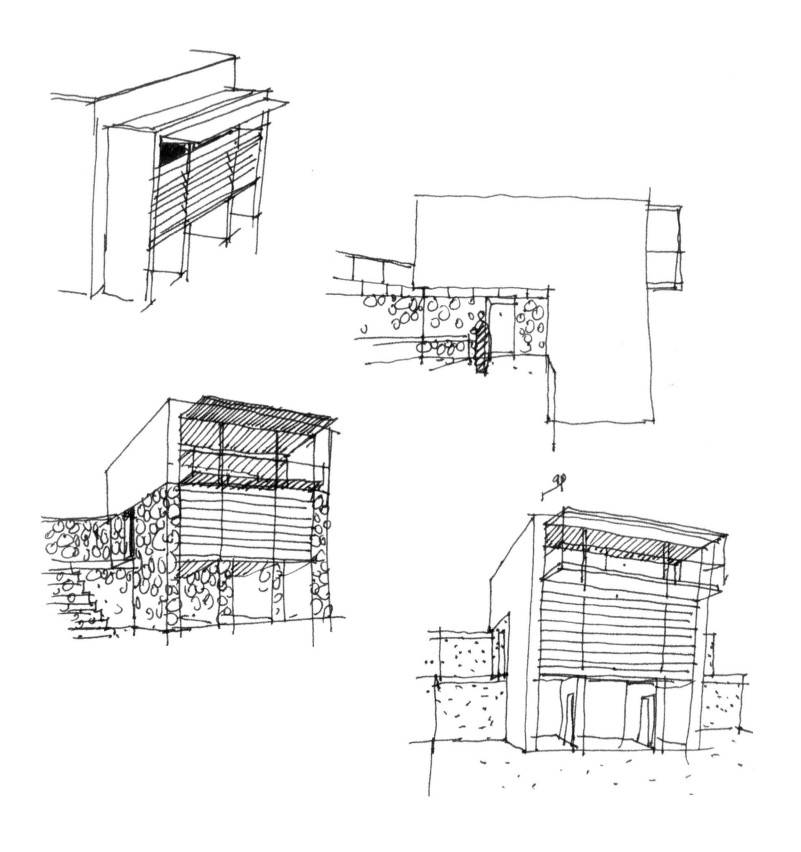

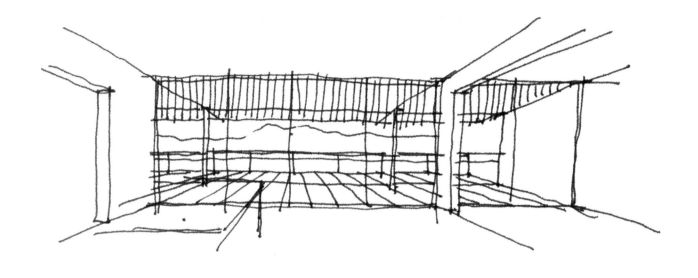

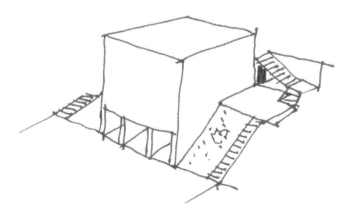

The structure of the house is conventional, with load-bearing walls and slabs, while the exterior finish has been rendered and painted. The enclosing elements are aluminum and the blinds are PVC; all railings are stainless steel and the entrance façade has been clad in a wood veneer.

Atelier Bow-Wow
Izu House

Shizuoka, Nishizu, Japan

The client wished to completely pull up stakes from his house in Tokyo and live at a more leisurely pace in a peaceful rural setting. Arriving at the chosen site, one leaves the main road and takes a narrow path through a former tangerine plantation, the view suddenly opening outward to the immensity of Suruga Bay 100 meters below. The site is abutted on one side by a sheer cliff, giving the impression of being almost in the sky and sea. This sensation is heightened by a pier structure protruding out over the cliff.

The preliminary architectural study focused on how to implant the dwelling on such a steep incline, while also bringing the adjacent tiered field into the design scheme. At the same time, the client insisted that he did not want a home nestled too snugly into the landscape, preferring instead to challenge his corporal senses and arouse a feeling of being headed for the future. The final plan consists of a gravity-defying pier as well as a firm psychological connection to terra firma via the garden.

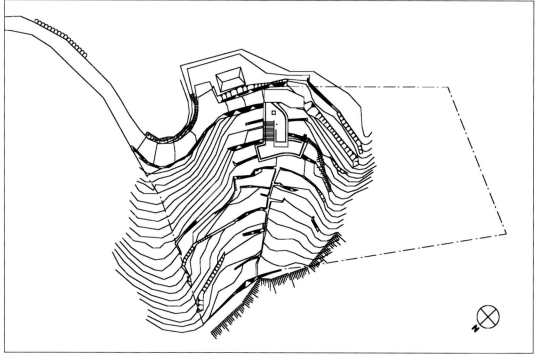

Photographs: Takashi Homma

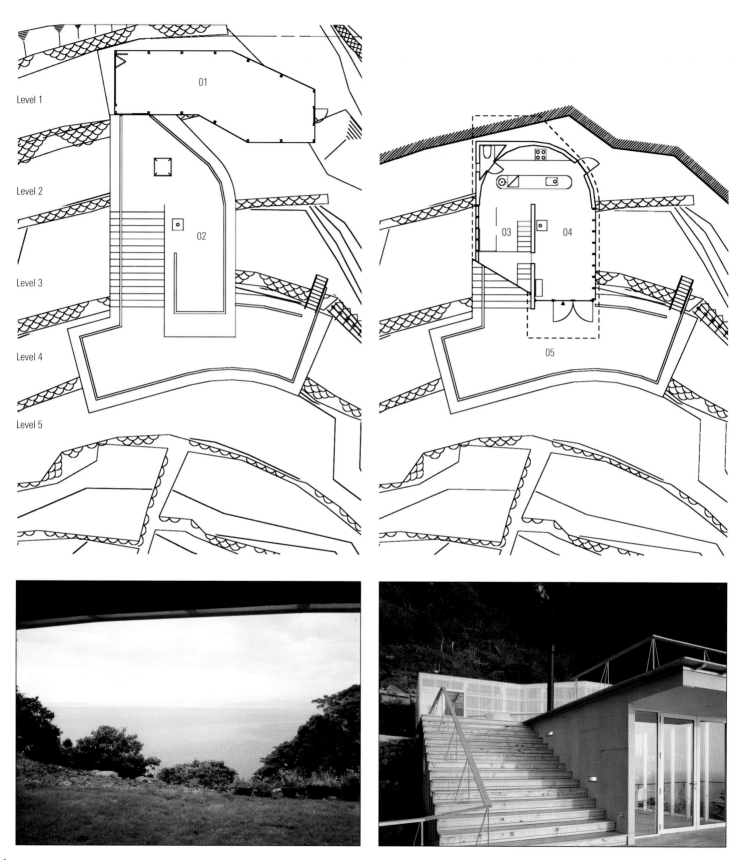

Level 1

Level 2

Level 3

Level 4

Level 5

01

02

03 04

05

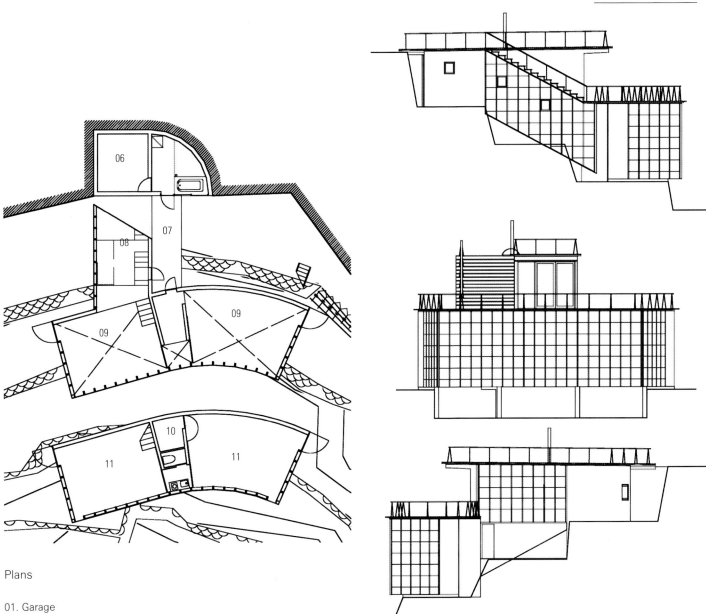

Plans

01. Garage
02. Roof terrace
03. Bedroom
04. Living
05. Roof terrace
06. Closet
07. Passage
08. Bedroom
09. Study
10. Closet
11. Atelier

Elevations

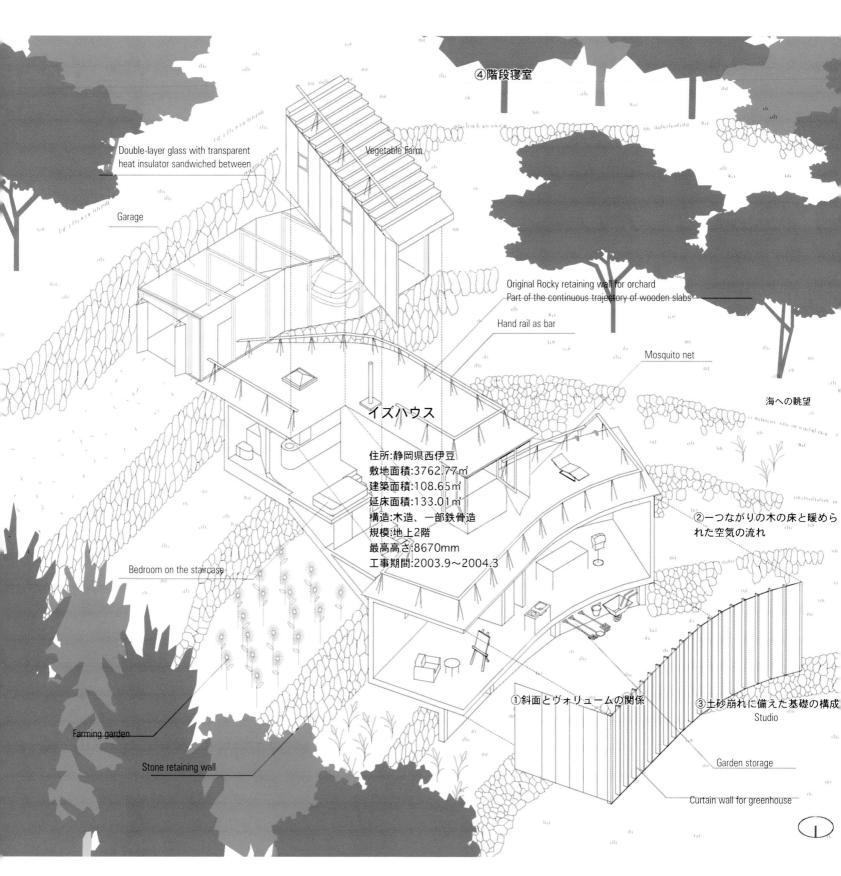

④階段寝室

Double-layer glass with transparent
heat insulator sandwiched between

Vegetable Farm

Garage

Original Rocky retaining wall for orchard
Part of the continuous trajectory of wooden slabs

Hand rail as bar

Mosquito net

海への眺望

イズハウス

住所:静岡県西伊豆
敷地面積:3762.77㎡
建築面積:108.65㎡
延床面積:133.01㎡
構造:木造、一部鉄骨造
規模:地上2階
最高高さ:8670mm
工事期間:2003.9〜2004.3

②一つながりの木の床と暖められた空気の流れ

Bedroom on the staircase

①斜面とヴォリュームの関係

③土砂崩れに備えた基礎の構成
Studio

Farming garden

Garden storage

Stone retaining wall

Curtain wall for greenhouse

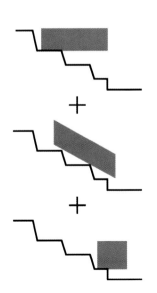

+

+

1. Slope of hill and house volume

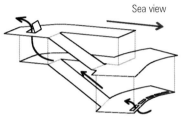

Sea view

2. Air flows along the continuous wooden slabs

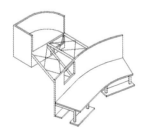

3. Foundation is designed to withstand landslides

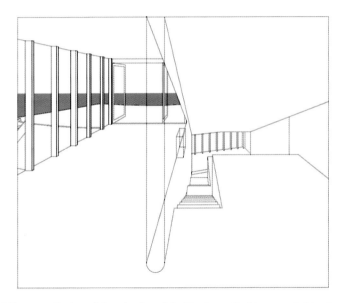

4. The stepped bedroom follows the slope of the hill, whereas the living room stretches towards the sea

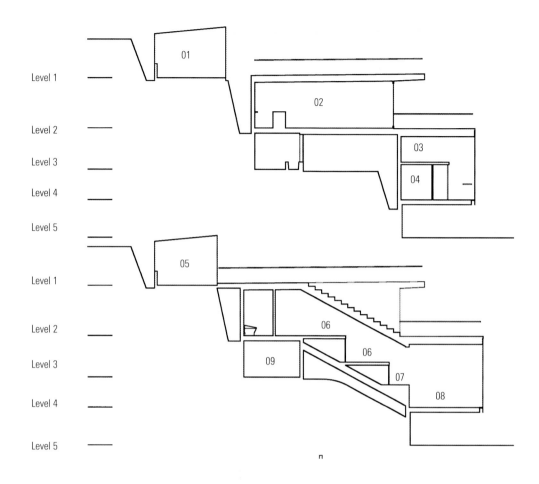

Level 1

01

Level 2

02

Level 3

03

Level 4

04

Level 5

Level 1

05

Level 2

06

Level 3

09

06

07

Level 4

08

Level 5

Sections

01. Garage
02. Living
03. Study
04. Closet
05. Garage
06. Bedroom
07. Study
08. Atelier
09. Closet

Izu House
Location: Nishi-izu, Shizuoka Prefecture, Japan
Structure: Timber and steel frame
Vertical composition: Two floors above ground
Site area: 763 m²
Footprint: 109 m²
Total floor area: 133 m²
Maximum height: 8.7 meters
Completion: March 2004

Buzacott Associates Architects
Hart/Picknett House

Killcare, NSW, Australia

The original house was a three-level, brick veneer 1970's house built on the side of a steep ridge overlooking Killcare Beach, an hour and half's drive north of Sydney. The architects found the house in a very dilapidated condition due to faulty construction; it was also poorly laid out, with small pokey rooms that did not take full advantage of its position. The existing decks were in a dangerous condition and the existing pool area to the west of the house was inaccessible directly from the interior.

The brief called for the opening up of the top level to provide open living spaces set between an enlarged eastern deck facing the beach and the rebuilt pool area on the western side of the house on the entry level. Four bedrooms and two bathrooms were required on the mid level and a separate apartment in the shell of the unbuilt lowest level.

As the current planning code would not allow a new house to achieve the same volume and height as the original construction, the architects decided to work within the constraints of the existing design, trimming and adjusting to achieve a more balanced building.

The house is entered from the western side via the existing drive and new pergola structure.

From the drive there is a small entry courtyard that leads either directly to the pool deck and a terrace off the kitchen or the formal entry at the half level between the two upper floors. An open stair leads up to the main living floor which has been totally opened into one large space (12x6 meters).

The main living space has large sliding doors onto a new steel framed balcony facing the beach and projecting out over the trees below. An open kitchen links around to the redesigned pool terraces to the west. Three new south-facing windows have been opened up along the kitchen end of the house. A new loft/study space above the garage overlooks the living space.

A major element of the redesign is a dramatic steel-framed structure that supports the three new deck levels and redesigned eastern facade. This steel structure was extended to support the roof and was tied back into the rock foundation. The structure is supported on cantilevered beams with the rake allowing for three decks widening out to the main upper deck with its central section cantilevering out further to allow for an outdoor dining space. The original klinker bricks have been color rendered and the house re-roofed with colored corrugated steel roofing.

Photographs: Adrian Boddy

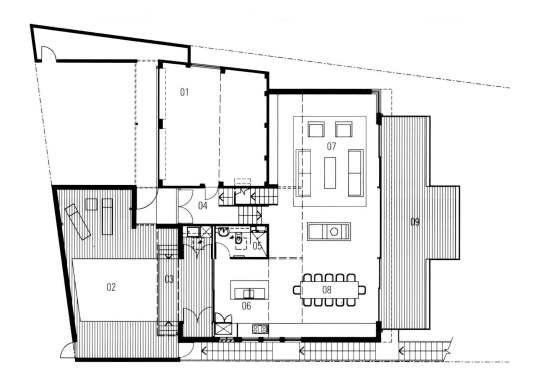

3rd floor plan - entrance

01. Garage
02. Pool
03. Laundry
04. Entry
05. Bath
06. Kitchen
07. Living
08. Dining
09. Deck

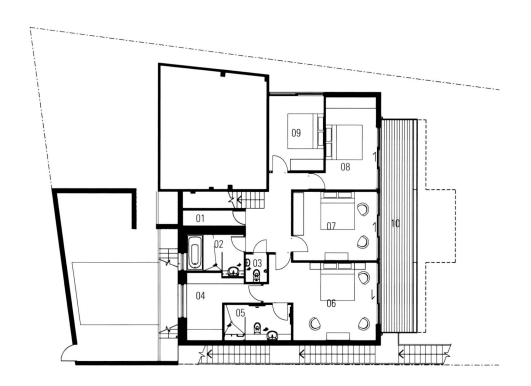

2nd floor plan

01. Store
02. Bath
03. WC
04. Dressing
05. Bath
06. Bedroom 1
07. Bedroom 2
08. Bedroom 3
09. Bedroom 4
10. Deck

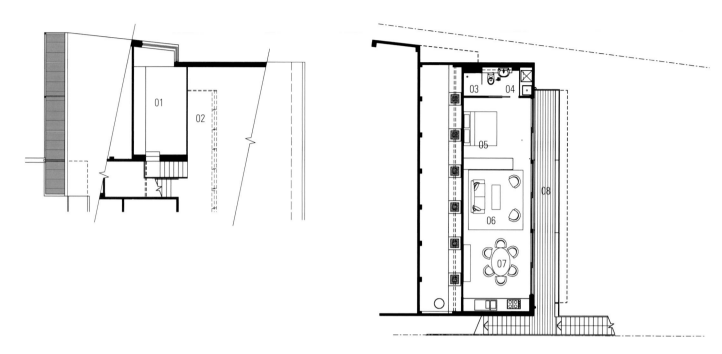

4th and 1st floor plan

01. Loft
02. Void
03. Bath
04. Laundry
05. Bedroom
06. Kitchen
07. Living
08. Deck

Section

01. Living
02. Bedroom
03. Flat
04. Hall
05. Entry
06. Pool

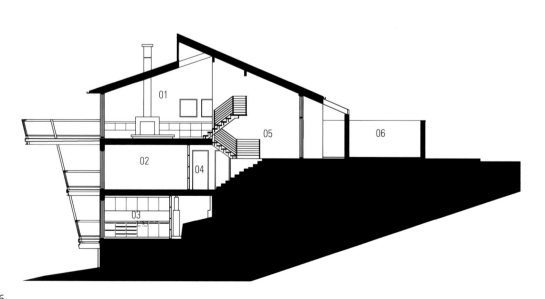

Barclay & Crousse
Equis House

La Escondida, Cañete, Peru

In carving out a place to live in the desert of the Peruvian coastline – an infinite void where the sea might be perceived as nothing more than an extension of it – the architects proposed a design that would 'domesticate' the 'absolute order' of the desert landscape, while making sure not to undermine or deny it.

To meet this end, a double strategy was decided upon: the maximum occupation of the built volume, and the definition of this occupation by a 'solid' (not just volumetric) body.

The result is a pure prism which has been pushed into the dunes, appearing almost as if it had always been there. This 'pre-existing' solid was 'excavated' throughout the design process, extracting material in order to simultaneously create and reveal its spaces in a subtractive logic that permeated all levels of the project.

The home is accessed via a threshold that both joins and separates the infinite space of the desert with/from the intimacy of the entrance courtyard. The courtyard stretches toward the ocean in the form of a large terrace designed as a sort of 'artificial beach' and a long, narrow lap pool, thus striking a relationship with the sea and the horizon. The roof, a large horizontal plane that encompasses the width of the plot, frames the seascape and brings together the living/dining room, which is separated from the terrace by a sliding, tempered glass partition.

A stairway following the slope of the land links the entry level to the bedrooms beneath the massive terrace. An intermediate landing distributes the rest of the bedrooms, which are protected from the sun by the overhanging terrace deck. At the end of the stairway, the lap pool is suspended over a balcony overlooking the sea; from here, one gains entrance to the master bedroom.

The ochre/sand tones, frequently used in pre-Columbian/pre-colonial constructions along the Peruvian coastline, ameliorate the 'visual ageing' effects brought about by dust deposits that saturate homes in the area, having been carried by the desert wind.

The great distance between the Parisian architectural studio and the actual site of the project necessitated a tremendous rationalization of the constructive system. All details were reduced to the essential and simplified in order to facilitate construction using a local crew without the need for direct supervision.

Photographs: J.P. Crousse

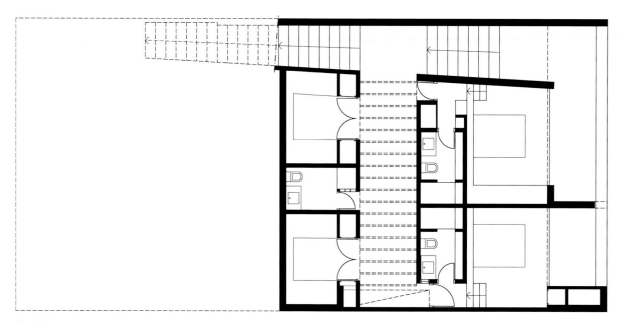

First floor

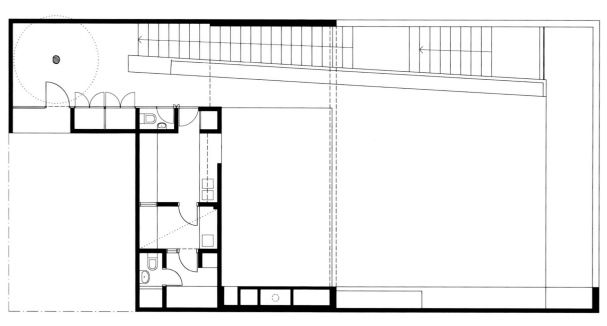

Second floor

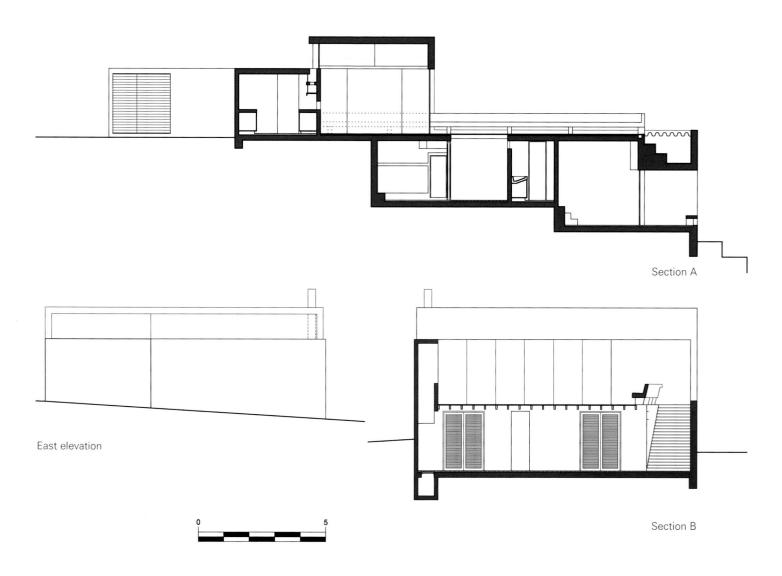

Section A

East elevation

Section B

0   5

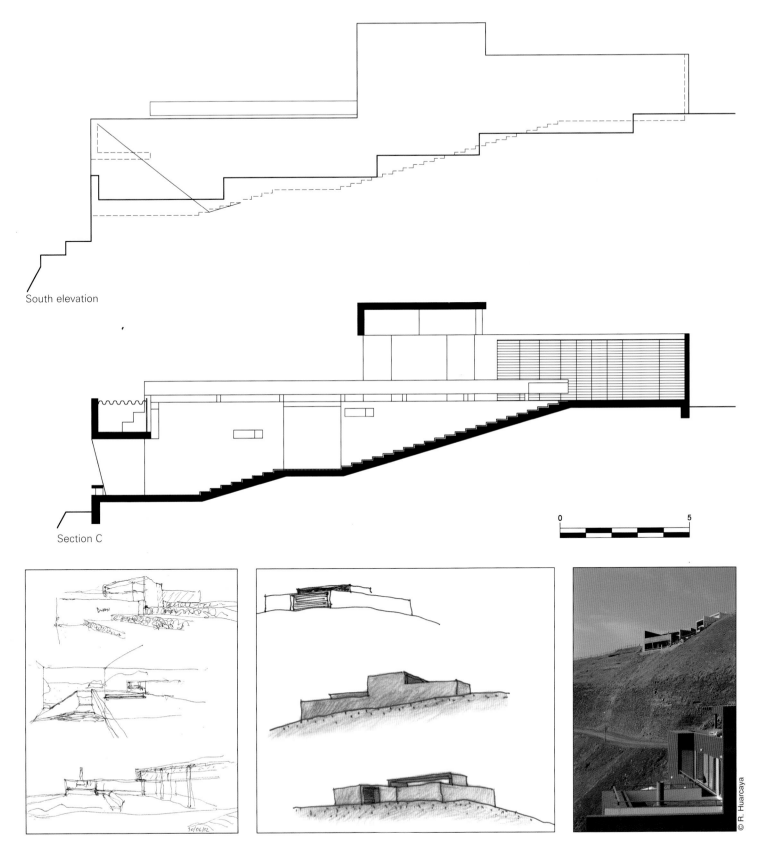

South elevation

Section C

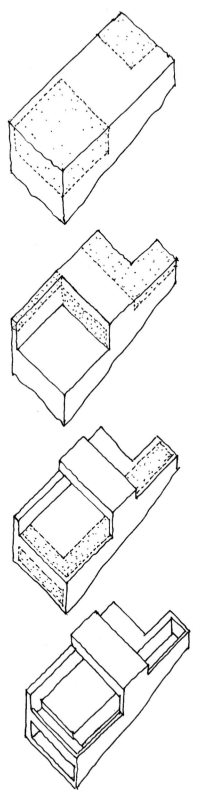

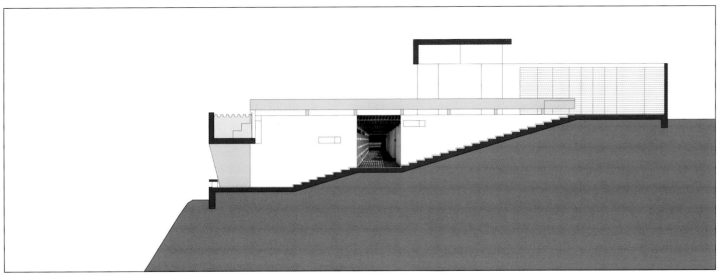

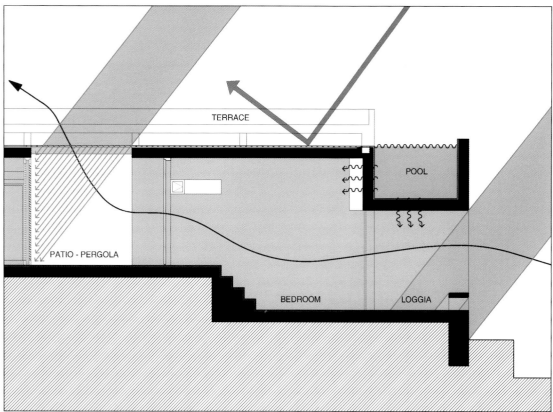

TERRACE

POOL

PATIO - PERGOLA

BEDROOM

LOGGIA

The architects decided to create the necessary intimacy for inhabiting the desert, the end result being worked into this landscape that is so powerful, yet at the same time sensitive to the objects that alter its omnipresent order.

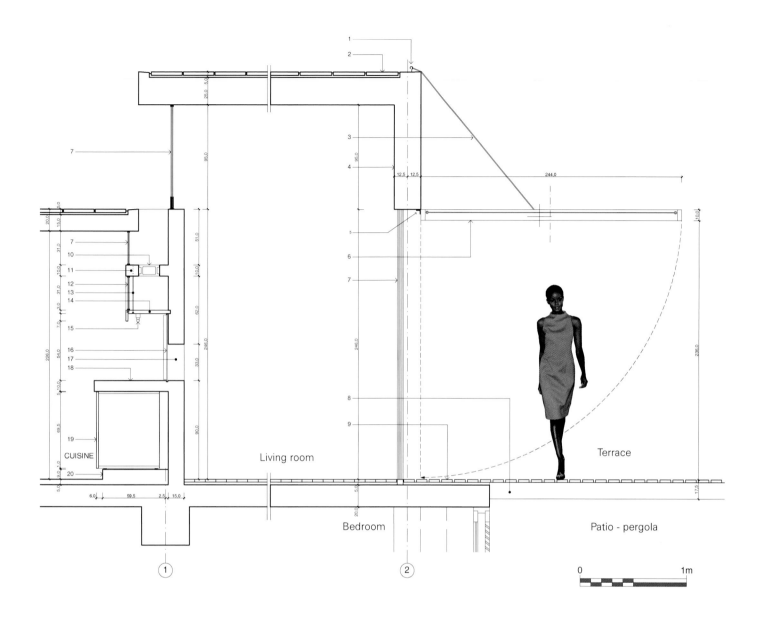

CUISINE

Living room

Bedroom

Terrace

Patio - pergola

0   1m

1. Fixtures of stainless steel

2. Terracotta tiles 30 x 30

3. Nylon cord- - tenser

4. Concrete beam, rendered and painted white

5. Hinge

6. PIVOTING SUN SHIELD:
structure of lacquered aluminum + permeable textile

7. Sliding panels of tempered glass

8. Wooden beam 15x 5 cm

9. Wooden slats 10 x 4 cm, spaced every 2 cm

10. Glass bricks 20 x 20

11. Painted concrete tiles

12. Sliders of translucent glass

13. Structural support of the furniture piece

14. Tall piece of furniture in painted medium

15. Warm tone fluorescent light

16. Sliding hatch in painted medium

17. Passe-plats

18. Work surface in polished cement

19. Stainless steel door

20. Floor and plinth in polished cement

The ambiguity between the closed and open spaces within the building and the surrounding grounds was enhanced to the maximum; each zone is qualified by its distinct relationship with the sky or the sea.

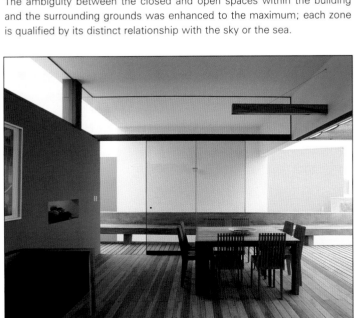